PHOTOGRAPHS

OF

ARCHITECTURE AND SCENER

PHOTOGRAPHS

OF

ARCHITECTURE AND SCENER

IN

GUJARAT AND RAJPUTANA

PHOTOGRAPHED BY

BOURNE AND SHEPHERD.

JAMES BURGESS, F.R.G.S., M.R.A.S.

GYAN

Published by

GYAN

Gyan Publishing House
5, Ansari Road
Daryaganj, New Delhi-110002
Phone: 011-47034999, 9811692060
E-mail: books@gyanbooks.com

Distribution Network
gyanbooks.com
India, USA, Canada, UK, Australia, France

ISBN : 978-81-212-9446-1 (PB)
First Published, 1874

2nd Impression 2023

Printed at: Gyan Press, Delhi.

PHOTOGRAPHS OF ARCHITECTURE AND SCENER
Author: JAMES BURGESS

I. AHMEDABAD—RÂNÎ SIPRÎ'S MOSK AND TOMB.

PHOTOGRAPHS

OF

ARCHITECTURE AND SCENERY

IN

Gujarat and Rajputana.

PHOTOGRAPHED BY

BOURNE AND SHEPHERD.

WITH HISTORICAL AND DESCRIPTIVE LETTERPRESS BY

JAMES BURGESS, F.R.G.S., M.R.A.S.,

Editor of "The Indian Antiquary," Author of "The Rock-Temples of Elephanta," "The Temples of Śatrunjaya," &c.

Calcutta, Bombay, and Simla:

BOURNE AND SHEPHERD.

1874.

CONTENTS.

SINCE the Daniells first published their large volumes of Views of Architecture, &c. in India, about the commencement of the century, a growing taste has been slowly spreading among Europeans for works illustrative of the Architecture, Scenery, Races, Costumes, &c., of the great Eastern dependency of our Empire. This has been partially met and fostered by such publications as Grindlay's "Views," &c., "The Indian Portfolio," Fergusson's "Rock-Cut Temples," and "Picturesque Illustrations of Indian Architecture," and, more recently, by numerous works illustrated by photography.

The belief that a selection of views from Gujarat and Rajputana would meet with public support, and help to spread a knowledge of the beauties of Indian Architecture and Scenery, has led the publishers to put forth the present volume of photographs, selected from a larger series taken by Mr. C. Murray, partner of the firm, during a tour in these provinces in the months of December 1872, January, February, and March 1873. I accompanied him, for the benefit of my health, through Ahmedabad, Pahlanpur, and the miserable remains of Chandravati, to Mount Abu, and thence through Sirohi to Sâdrî, by the Desurî Pass across the Arâvali Hills, to Komalmer, Kailwâ, Râjnagar, Nâthdwâra, Dilwâḍâ, and Eklinga to Udaypur, and then to Chittur, where, leaving Mr. Murray to go by Bhainsrorgaḍh, Baroli, Kotâ, Bundi, Deolî, Rajmahal and Bisalpur to Ajmer, I went direct to Ajmer and Puskar *en route* for Jaypur and Agra. Instead of drawing entirely on my own notes for the materials of the letterpress, which would thereby have been more antiquarian in character, I have designedly drawn largely on the masterly criticisms of Mr. J. Fergusson in his *Picturesque Illustrations of Ancient Architecture in Hindostan*, and *History of Architecture*,—works of the highest interest to every student of the History of Oriental Architecture, and from which I have been kindly permitted to use some of the woodcuts. I have also availed myself of the accounts of Tod, Heber, and Jacquemont, and the references appended to some of the articles will help the reader to fuller sources of information respecting many of the places noticed. I regret that these notes have been written so hurriedly, and without the care I could have otherwise wished to bestow on a subject so interesting and attractive.

JAS. BURGESS.

Edinburgh, 15 *Dec.* 1873.

II. AHMEDABAD—WINDOW AND BASE OF MINARET IN RANI SPIRI'S MOSK.

ARCHITECTURE AND SCENERY

IN

GUJARAT AND RAJPUTANA.

AHMEDABAD.

AHMEDABAD was at one time the most splendid city in India; the circumference of its suburbs was about twenty-seven miles, and its population two million souls. Gujarat had been wrested by Ala ud-dîn from the Wâghela kings in 1297, and placed under Muhammadan Governors. In 1397 the Mughul scourge, Kutb ud-dîn Amîr Tîmûr Gûrgân Çahib-kiran—the great Timurlang—swept down upon Dehli with his merciless hordes, and overthrew the Tughlak dynasty. The Governor of Gujarat was Muhammad Shah Zaffar Khân, the son of Waji ul Mulk, a convert from the Tâka clan of Râjputs, who, like many other provincial governors at the time, assumed independence and founded the dynasty of Gujarat,—which held sway till 1572, distinguished alike for its military enterprise, the destruction of Hindu fanes, and its architectural works in mosks, tombs, and palaces.

In 1410 Muzaffar was poisoned by his grandson Ahmad Shah, and next year, at the instigation of Sheikh Ahmad Kattu Ganj Bakhsh, his spiritual adviser, Ahmad founded this city, as his new capital, beside the old Hindu town of Aśâwal, which formed one of the *mahallas* or wards in its suburbs. "The situation," says Abu'l Fazl, writing in the end of the sixteenth century, "is remarkably healthy, and you may here provide yourself with the productions of every part of the globe. There are two forts, on the outside of which is the town, which formerly consisted of 360 *puras* (or quarters), but now only 84 are in a flourishing condition. In these are a thousand stone masjids, each having two large minarets and many wonderful inscriptions." Each *mahalla*, Ferishtah tells us, had a wall surrounding it; the principal streets were sufficiently wide to admit of ten carriages abreast; and "on the whole," he says, "this is the handsomest city in Hindustan, and perhaps in the world." But the Hindu cities of Anhillawâḍâ Paṭṭan and Chandrâvatî had been dilapidated to raise it, and the work of reconstruction was accomplished by aid of the wonderful perseverance and skill of the Hindu *śilpi* or mason. No wealth or taste was spared on the mosks and tombs of its Sultans, their families, grandees, and favourite slaves. To give any account of even the principal of those in the city and vicinity, at Batwâ, Shah Âlam, and Sarkhej, would fill a volume: we can only give a specimen :—

The Rânî Sîprî ki masjîd.

Photographs I. *and* II.

This is near the Astoria Gate on the south-east side of the city. Unfortunately, its position prevents its being seen to advantage: it stands with its south-west corner to the street, which is much lower than the platform on which both it and the mausoleum stand. Rânî Sîprî was the wife of one of the sons of Ahmad Shah, and doubtless the daughter of some Hindu chief; and, as was usually the case, the tomb and its necessary adjunct the mosk were probably built by herself during her lifetime. They were completed Anno Hejira 835 (*i.e.* A.D. 1432).

The mosk is a hall, open to the east, about 54 feet in length over all, and 20 feet wide. The roof is supported by two rows of six double columns, and the towers at the front corners are about 50 feet high.

" Notwithstanding the smallness of its dimensions," says Mr. Fergusson, "it may be considered the gem of Ahmedabad, and, in its class, as one of the most exquisite buildings in the world. It is also one of the most perfectly Hindu of the buildings of this city, no arch being employed anywhere (except in one side doorway), either constructively or for ornament. The minarets, too, though so exquisite in design, are not minarets in reality; they have no internal stairs, and no galleries from which the call to prayer could be recited: they are pure ornaments, but of the most graceful kind. The charm of this building resides in two things. First, the completeness and unity of the design: every form and every detail is designed for the place where it is put, and is appropriate to that place. And next, to the fact that all the details are beautiful in themselves, and just sufficient to relieve and accentuate the construction, without ever concealing or interfering with it. It would of course be absurd to compare such a building with the Parthenon, or one of our great Gothic cathedrals; but it is, architecturally, a more perfect building than the Erechtheion at Athens; and though we have some Gothic chapels of great beauty, there probably is not one that would not look coarse and plain if placed side by side with this mosk." * Elsewhere, the same writer remarks of the minarets that they are "still more beautiful" than those of Cairo, and that every part of the mosk "is such as only a Hindu Queen could order, and only Hindu artists could carve." †

The view given in the Photograph (No. I.) is taken from the north-east, and shows about half the front of the mosk, with a portion of the tomb,—also a fine building of its kind, but unfortunately much dilapidated, and large portions of the open stone lattice-work in the walls damaged or destroyed.

The two windows in the south end, facing the street (Photo. No. II.), are genuine Hindu or Jaina in style and minutest detail: thrown well out on elaborately carved brackets, and shaded above by projecting stone eaves, they are admirably adapted to reduce the bright glare of a tropical clime, and while admitting sufficient light and air, they suggest a feeling of coolness.

The base of the south-east minaret is shown in the same view; it also is Hindu in plan and the main features of its details. In plan it is a miniature of what we find repeated in endless variety in the shrines of Western India. In Hindu and Jaina temples, however, the niches and faces of the re-entrant angles are ornamented with images of their *devatas;* any image of living thing the Muslim could not endure, and so here, on the base, above the principal niche, and again in the upper niche, instead of the Jaina figure of a bell hanging by a chain, we have the Musalman lamp similarly suspended; and in the principal niches we have for an architectural detail an ingeniously wrought, conventionalised flower tracery. The mosks of Ahmedabad are famous for forms of this kind—some of the best being in the Queen's mosk at Mirzapur, in the Shahpura mosk, and in the Bhadr. Speaking of these details, Mr. Fergusson remarks that: "After a century's experience they (the Muhammadans at Ahmedabad) produced forms which, as architectural ornaments, will, in their own class, stand comparison with any employed in any age or in any part of the world.‡"

---

* *Architecture of Ahmedabad*, pp. 84, 85.

† *History of Architecture*, vol. ii. p. 674.

‡ *History of Architecture*, vol. ii. p. 671.

III. ADÂLAJ—THE PUBLIC WELL OR WÂV.

THE WÂV OR PUBLIC WELL AT ADÂLAJ.

Photograph III.

ABOUT twelve miles north of Ahmedabad is the village of Adâlaj, where is to be seen one of the finest public wells or *wâvs* in Gujarat. A WÂV is a large well, usually consisting of two parts—a well, often octagonal, from which the water is drawn up in skins, by bullocks, the ropes passing over rude pulleys on the upper edge of the well; and secondly, of a wide staircase by which the women descend to the level of the water, there to fill their water-pots. These *wâvs* are common all over Gujarat and Rajputana: thus there is one a little farther north than this, at Dnyanoj; and at Asârwâ, a suburb to the north-east of Ahmedabad, there is a very old one known as Mâtâ Bhavâni's; and another near by, built in A.D. 1499 by Śri Harira, a Hindu lady of the harem of Mahmud Begaḍhâ. This latter is the only one in the province that can compare with the Adâlaj wâv, and the latter has probably been the finer of the two. The platform at the head of the descent to the water is reached by short flights of steps in front and on each side. This platform is on a level with the first or upper gallery, and from it the stair—the whole width of the *wâv*—descends by eight or nine steps to a narrow platform, and from it again to a third, down through the three galleries; the water standing in the cold season about the level of the platform or floor of the last. The platforms, except the first and portions of the well of similar area, are roofed over in each gallery; the stairs and corresponding portions of the well are open to the sky. These partial floorings form a support for the columns in the different galleries, and the whole construction is a most effective and elegant support to the side walls against the pressure of the earth behind. The first platform is a square, partially roofed over at the corners, leaving an octagonal opening above, which may possibly have been intended to be covered by a dome. The columns bear a striking resemblance to those in Rânî Sipri's Masjid, differing only in the want of one member in the base, but they are much heavier in proportion to their height.

In the window-like niches, and on a band of sculpture that runs right round the walls of the upper gallery, figures of elephants, and other animals, have been introduced; but on the second pair of pillars, and their corresponding pilasters, the faces of the shafts are ornamented by the lamp hanging by a chain from a rosette, and surrounded by a floral design, exactly similar to what we find in niches, and even in the *mehrâbs* of the masjids at Ahmedabad. Between these pillars, and between them again and the pilasters, there have once been *toranas*,—those ornamental arches so frequent in the Châlukya style of architecture.

The cornice that projects under the base of the pilasters enables one to scramble along the whole of the galleries, and on the right side of the upper gallery, in a niche, is found a Sanskrit inscription, of which the following is an outline translation:*—

"Samvat 1555 (A.D. 1498), month of Mâgha, Mahmud Padshah being king.

"Salutation to Vinayaka (*Ganeśa*,) to whose race belonged King Mokala, chief of the country of Dandâhi. From him was born Karṇa, whose son was Mûla-râja. Mahîpa was Mûla-râja's son, and Virasinha and Naisha were the sons of Mahîpa. Vîrasinha's queen, whose name is Rûjhâ, has constructed this well. It is dedicated at this time—when the sun is in the north, the month is Mâgha, the bright half (*śukla paksha*), the 5th day, the day of the week, Wednesday, the lunar mansion—Uttarâ, Karaṇa-Bava, the yoga—Siddhi."

Then follows a glowing description of the well, after which the queen, or rather lady of the chief, is praised in a few verses; the expense is stated at 5,00,111 ṭankas, or over five lakhs, and the whole ends with a repetition of the date as given above.

---

* This has been prepared by Professor Ramkrishna Gopal Bhandarkar, M.A.

THE RUDRA MÂLÂ AT SIDDHPUR.

Photograph IV.

ABOUT sixty-five miles north of Ahmedabad, prettily situated on a rising ground on the north bank of the river sacred to Sarasvatî, "the watery," stands the town of Siddhpur. Here the stream, which generally flows in a south-westerly direction, makes a bend towards the east, facing the rising sun, and is there regarded as of peculiar sanctity. Thus the bard sings of it :—

Tirath bhumipâvan Siddhakshetra subhasâr,
Nirmâl nir vahe Sarasvatî sada mokshko dwâr, &c.—

"A *Tirtha*, a place to make holy, is the good Siddha Kshetra,
Where flows Sarasvatî's pure stream—ever beatitude's door.
A city three worlds to purify, by Siddhs ever worshipped,
Gods, Rishis, and men cherish the desire to live there.
And there dwell *devas* unnumbered, as a *tirtha* regarding it,—
Of Kâsi, Gâya, Godâvarî, and all other *tirthas*, the best;
Where Kardam and Dehuti lived, and Kapila was born.
Here is Bindusarovar's pure fount, and Matrugayâ;
Applied to the bodies of men degraded and fallen, it washes their myriads of sins.
Here is Prâchi Mahâdev, whose renown by Ved and Purâna is sung :
Of all *Tirthas*, the essence—it is named Kapilashrâm."

The olden name of this holy place appears to have been *Śrîsthala*, and in the tenth century (A.D. 943) Mula Râja, the founder of the Solanki dynasty of Gujarat, began to embellish it by the erection of the *Rudra Mâlâ*, a famous temple of Śiva, of which the gigantic fragments that still remain, interspersed among the houses of one of the dirtiest towns of Western India, impress the beholder with admiration at the scale and grandeur of the conception. In his youth Mula Deva had slain his maternal uncle, usurped his throne, and murdered the whole of his mother's kindred; and in old age his crimes hung heavily on his mind. He made pilgrimages and courted the favour of Brahmans from far and near. To a band of them he gave *Śrîsthala*, and committing the kingdom to his son Châmund, he retired thither to end his days in their company (A.D. 996). But the Rudra Mâlâ was still incomplete, nor was it finished till A.D. 1145. Colonel Tod mentions an inscription to this effect, and in a *Kavita* or ballad, already quoted, there occurs almost a literal version of it :—

"In Samvat ten (?) hundred, begun by Mahârâj Mûladev,
In Samvat twelve hundred and two, Siddharâj completed the work;
In Samvat twelve hundred two, Mâgh month, Krishna paksh,
On Monday the fourteenth, in the Nakshatra Śrâvan and Varyan Yoga,
Siddharâj, in the Rudra Mâl, Śivashankar established."

To Siddharâja and his mother, Mainâl Devi, tradition attributes the erection of many splendid edifices, and is doubtless correct in so doing: it was truly the Augustan age of architecture in Gujarat; but to what circumstance we owe the completion of the stupendous pile begun by his ancestor we cannot tell. Legend says two Parmârs from Mâlwâ, named Govindâs and Mâdhavdâs, took up their haunt among the rush grass that covered the neighbourhood of the Rudra Mâlâ, and lived by plunder. There they found the foundations of a temple and a *Śiva linga*, and said that in the night they had seen *devas* and *apsârasas*, or heavenly maids. This was told to Siddharâja, and led to the erection of the great fane.

IV. SIDDHPUR—RUINS OF THE RUDRA MALA.

"The Râja," writes Ali Muhammad Khan, "on signifying his intention of building the above-mentioned temple, requested the astrologers, it is said, to appoint a fortunate hour; and they at this time predicted the destruction of the building" by a Muslim invader. Then Siddha Râja caused images of "horse lords" and other great kings to be placed in the temple, and "near them a representation of himself in the attitude of supplication, with an inscription praying that, even if the land was laid waste, this temple might not be destroyed."* Then was the name of *Śrîsthala* changed for that of *Siddhapur*, in commemoration of his restoration of the city and shrine.†

But the evil day came: Ala-ud-din Khilji, surnamed *Khuni*, or "the Bloody," ascended the throne of Dehli in 1296, and sent an army under Almas Beg Alaf Khân and Nusrat Khân Jalesri, and "fulfilled the obligations of the law by converting the temple into a *masjid* with minars." Tod quotes a couplet recording its destruction. "In Samvat 1353 (A.D. 1296), came the barbarian Ala: the Rudra-Mâla he levelled, carrying destruction amongst the lords of men."

The principal fragments that now remain of this once splendid shrine are five in number,—shut in among houses, which have been built over the greater part of the area it once occupied. The *Kirti Stambha*, or triumphal arch—which was nearly perfect only a few years ago—has now been denuded of the principal sculptures in the pediment, and of the beautiful *toran* or garland-like arch that sprung from the capitals of the columns and touched the architrave above,—the architrave itself resting on dwarf columns that rise from the capitals of the great pillars. From the ground to the architrave is about twenty-four feet; the pediment rises perhaps ten feet above this; and the whole has been finished in the most ornate style of Hindu art. It is now much defaced about the base of the pillars, but it still strikes the visitor as having been a noble piece of masonry. Twelve yards south from it stand five massive columns, which appear to have formed the east or front porch of the great temple and a pillar of its doorway. They are surmounted by lintels, and still retain their *toranas;* whilst over the inner pair of the portico rise two pillars of the second story, also still supporting their architrave. Other columns may have fallen or been pulled down within the last fifty years, for Tod, in 1822, describes this as "a mass of two stories, each supported by four columns, and the columns of a third story, preserving, without any entablature, their perfect perpendicularity." A huge block lies diagonally across the lintel of the outer columns, and I was told it had fallen there during the earthquake of 1819, which, as Colonel Tod learnt, had "thrown down two of the loftiest columns." ‡

On the bases which support the pillars at the entrance there are inscriptions,—one of them dated in A.D. 1249. A third portion of these ruins, to the west of the last, consists of four columns in a line, the upper sections of them elaborately carved, and not much defaced. A portion of this fragment appears on the right hand in the plate. The base, shaft, capital, and bracket of each is a single stone, and over the four lies an architrave, consisting of a single block about four feet square and twenty-six feet in length. Above this are two string courses, and then two plain columns on square bases with rough, square, bracket capitals supporting a lintel under which runs a wooden beam. The height of this is 38 feet; and if the temple was of three stories, as Tod's statements would lead us to conclude it must have been, the *mandap* may have been about sixty feet in height; but tradition reports variously that it had five, six, or even *seven* stories.

Between this and the *Kirti Stambha* are four pillars (appearing on the left in the plate) with three elaborate *toranas;* the architraves over them are also richly carved, as are the two pillars and two pilasters that surmount them, with the entablature above. Lastly, to the west of all the other fragments, is a mosk, consisting of three low domes, apparently the porticoes to three of the small shrines which probably surrounded the court of the great temple. The columns have been elaborately carved, but all the small human figures have been hewn out, whilst over the domes may still be seen portions of two of the *śikhars* of the shrines; and a fourth small temple, adjoining these on the north, is still nearly entire.

* Bird's *Mirat Ahmadi*, p. 157. † Forbes, *Ras Mala*, vol. i. p 116.

‡ Tod, *Travels in Western India*, p. 141.

The *Kavita*, or metrical account of the Rudra Mâlâ, already referred to, is a lengthy compositi various metres, beginning with the praises of *Siddhakshetra* and passing to a grandiloquent account o greatness of Mûla Deva, the foundation of the *Rudra Mâlâ*, the wealth, virtues, and power of Siddha the grandeur of the *Rudra Mâlâ*, and its overthrow.

"Rudra Mâlâ shone like the Kailas of Sriva,
Gems, rubies and diamonds set in it sparkled like lamp-flames,
Covered with gold like the mountain of Meru;
Inlaid with gems were the doors of it,
Festoons filled with pearls were there;
Studded with screens and with lattices,
The *Mandaps* on its four sides were rendered attractive.

* * * * *

Pillars sixteen hundred adorned it,
Images eighteen thousand set with rubies and pearls,
Flags of gold tinsel floated, and pennons thirty thousand,
Kalases of gold, sixteen hundred decked it out,
Fifty-six lakhs of horses and elephants made a line,
Of carved screens a lakh and a quarter were there,
And of resting-places seven thousand two hundred;
Siddharâj Jésinha, for the Rudra Mâlâ Pratâd,
Fourteen karors of *mohors* for the cost, wrote down.

* * * * *

Four doors on four sides, and *Mandaps* three, I describe;
Other shrines all around it, numberless shine;
The varied labours appear to the eye most enchanting,
In the midst, to Great Rudra, eleven shrines he erected,
Siddhasinh with the Brahmans together there meeting,
For its name "Rudra Mâlâ" established,
Gananana in the midst sounds the drum, the cymbal *gananana*,
Gananana re-echoes the bell, till the ear is stunned with the sound."

In 1415 Ahmad Shah completed the destruction of the Rudra Mâlâ, and we hear little more Siddhapur till the monsoon of 1573, when the great Akbar, after taking possession of Gujarat, encampec it till Vaḍanagar had been taken and Aulia Khân seized by the troops, sent out for that purpose, un Râja Bhagwandâs. At that period Abu'l Fazl speaks of it as still "a great place of religious resort."

V. MOUNT ABU, THE NAKHI TALÂO, &c., FROM THE WEST.

MOUNT ABU.

Photograph V.

MOUNT ABU, in the territory of Sirohi in Rajputana, is about fifty miles N.N.E. from Siddhapur. Though usually regarded as part of the Aravali range, it is completely detached from that chain on all sides, and rises from the great plain of Mârwâr like an island from the level ocean. The ascent of this noble granite mountain is steep on all sides, and at the top it is surrounded by a wall of granite enclosing a plateau of considerable extent and largely covered with hills. The highest of these is Guru Śikhar, on the northern part of the plateau, which attains a height of 5,650 feet above the sea level.

In the thirteenth century Mount Abu was held by the Parmârs of Chandravati—vassals of the old Hindu kings of Gujarat. This Chandravati, a little to the south-east of Abu—once a splendid capital—is now only indicated by the many mounds of ruined temples and palaces that mark its site. The Muhammadan Sultans of Ahmedabad first, the Thakurs of Girwar more recently, and up to the present day the head men to whom the Sirohi Râo grants charge of the village, have carried away and burnt to lime its marble slabs, columns, and statues, and still continue to do so, until but few fragments are left except such as are covered by *débris*.

Abu, the ancient *Arbuda*, is usually ascended from Anâdrâ, on the south-west side, by a good road, but of steep ascent, rising about 3,000 feet in three miles. The first point reached on attaining the plateau—here from 3,900 to 4,000 feet above the sea level—is the little lake, of fairy beauty, called NAKHI TALAO—vulgarly translated the 'Nail Lake,' but more appropriately the 'Gem Lake.' Fifty years ago Tod described it as "about four hundred yards in length," and "the counterpart of the lake three miles above Andernach on the Rhine." "It is," he writes, "surrounded by rocks, wooded to the margin, while the waterfowls skim its surface unheeding and unheeded by man; for on this sacred hill, neither the fowler's gun nor fisher's net is known; 'Thou shalt not kill' being the supreme command, and the penalty of disobedience, death."* But great changes have taken place on Abu since 1822. The Governor-General's Agent for Rajputana spends the hot season and monsoon on Abu; it is a sanatarium for European troops, with extensive barracks; and the late Sir Henry Lawrence founded there one of his schools for the children of European soldiers. And, though the station and camp are only rented from the Deora Râo of Sirohi, the presence of so many Europeans on the hill has led to marked changes in the aspect of the scene around the Nakhi Talâo. It is still a charming lakelet, the walk round which affords the visitor a continually varying panorama of exquisite beauty. A *bănd*, or dam, has recently been built across the gorge at the west end where the overflow runs off, in order to increase the depth of the water, fears having been entertained that it might run dry, or nearly so, should an exceptionally light monsoon occur.†

There are several small islands with trees on them scattered about the Talâo, but they are almost submerged. A path has been made all round it, and it must be confessed that the straight lines of this, on the north-west side, somewhat mar the picturesqueness of some points of the view. Considerably above the lake on the south side is a path, known as Bailey's Walk—so named from the present magistrate, who made it—and which extends from the station at the east end of the lake to 'Sunset Point,' crossing over one of the higher peaks which overhang the lake. From the western parts of this Walk, on the one

---

* Tod, *Travels in Western India*, pp. 115, 116.

† See *Indian Antiquary*, vol. ii. pp. 249—257.

hand, the scene is over the spurs of Abu, and the vast plains of Mârwâr, and on the other we have a very fine view (given in the Photograph) across the lake to the north-east, where are seen the large blocks of barracks, and further to the east the Residency, and to the right of it the Office of the Governor-General's Agent; whilst under, and still further to the right, lie scattered the houses of the station.

The Station at Abu.

Photograph VI.

The Photograph, No. VI., is a view of part of the station as seen from the Residency; on the extreme left are the Offices of the Agency, and on the right is seen the roof and part of the west end of the little English church, nearly behind which is the Lawrence School, while between this and the Agency Offices, as also behind and before the School, are several bangalâs belonging to officers attached to the Agency. This picture gives a very fair idea of the station, charmingly situated on an undulating plateau surrounded by hills.

VI. MOUNT ABU, THE STATION, FROM THE RESIDENCY.

THE TEMPLES OF DELWADA.

Photographs VII. VIII.

MEMBERS of the Jain or Śrâvak sect are to be found in most of the large towns of the Lower Ganges and in Rajputana, but they are probably most numerous in Gujarat, Dhârwâḍ and Maisur. As their name implies, they are followers of the *Jinas*, or 'vanquishers' of sin—twenty-four men whom they believe to have obtained *nirvâna*, or emancipation from the changes of transmigration. With them *life*—which they do not distinguish from *soul*,—and its vehicle *matter*, are both uncreated and imperishable, obeying eternal physical laws, with which asceticism and religious ritual alone can interfere. Their ceremonial has, therefore, no real reference to a Supreme Personal God, and their doctrine excludes His providence. This points to their connection with the Buddhists; indeed, there can be little doubt that they owe their origin, at a very early date, to some heretical sect of the Hinayâna school of that persuasion, and probably owed in part their popularity, on the decline of the purer Bauddha doctrine, to their admission of the worship of some of the favourite Hindu divinities into their system and their retention of the tyranny of caste customs.*

From the tenth century, if not from an earlier date, the Jains have been distinguished as the builders of sumptuous temples to their JINAS or TIRTHANKARS. These temples have been raised chiefly at their sacred mounts, at Parasnâth in the west of Bengal, at Śatrunjaya in the east, and Girnar in the west of the peninsula of Kâthiâwâḍ, and here on Mount Abu. The most popular of these shrines, on which at the present day the greatest amount of wealth is lavished, is Śatrunjaya, near Pâlitânâ. It is covered with temples, many of them of very recent date, and of great beauty, and is altogether one of the most remarkable places in India.

Though Abu is not one of the greater Jaina *tîrthas*, or holy places, it can boast of at least two of the most beautiful of their temples in India. These are at Dêlwâḍâ, or *Devalwâḍâ*—'the place of temples'—about a mile north of the station. There are five temples here in all, one of the largest being a three-storied one, dedicated to Rishabhanâth, the first of the twenty-four Tirthankars, or deified men whom the Jains worship. The shrine, which is the only enclosed part of this temple, has four doors, one towards each of the cardinal points, and the image inside is quadruple—facing the four doors. This is called a *Chaumukh*, and is a not unfrequent form of the image of this Tirthankar :—

> "'Tis lifeless stone, a rayless, joyless dark
> Pourtrayed,—stagnation, death, the grave of thought!
> Yet here the worshipper hath come to gaze
> On men to gods transformed; hath come to bend
> Lowly as to his only God; he robbed
> His nature of each godlike relic left,
> Then worshipped the foul ruin of himself."†

On the west side the temple has a double *mandap* or portico, and on the other three sides single ones, each supported on eight columns. The corners between these domes are occupied by six more columns, which with the four columns added to each octagon to form the square, gives sixteen on each quarter between the lines of entrance. Over the square formed by the pillars on the lines of the inner sides of the octagons,

---

* For further information see *Indian Antiquary*, vol. ii. pp. 15, 16, 193—200, 261—265, &c., and Introduction to *The Temples of Śatrunjaya*, Bombay, 1869.

† "The Dilwârâ Temples of Abu," in the *Oriental Christian Spectator* for 1840, pp. 523—525.

rise the pillars of the second story, whilst the walls of the shrine are carried up to the roof. This form of shrine, with its four approaches, ample domes, and shady colonnades, is a fine type of the Jaina style of temple architecture, and from it, by very simple modifications, the other prevalent forms may easily be deduced.

To the north of Rishabhadeva's Chaumukh, and on a raised platform, is another large temple, without a spire, but with a roofed *mandap*, and which is locally known by the name of Bhenchaśah's.

To the S.E. by S. from the Chaumukh is a third temple, enclosed by a high wall, and known as Dailak, or the temple of Adiśvara (or Rishabhanâth) and Gorakhalanchan.

But it is to the west of the Chaumukh that the two finest temples are,—that known as Vimalaśah's dedicated to Adiśvara, the first Tirthankar, and opposite it, on the north side, is the temple of Vastupâla and Tejapâla, dedicated to Neminâtha, the twenty-second of the Tirthankars. The date of the former seems to be given in an inscription, hitherto undeciphered, but in which has been read the sentence,—

"Samvat 1088 (A.D. 1031), by the blessing of Ambâ, Vimalaśah built the temple of Adinâtha : this plate records its repair in Samvat 1379 (A.D. 1322), on Monday the ninth of the light fortnight of Jyeshth."

Several inscriptions over the shrines around the court are dated in Samvat 1245 (A.D. 1188), and record their dedication to Śântinâth, the sixteenth, and Aranâth, the eighteenth Tirthankar, by "Yasodhavala, of the race of Prâgvâta," or his family.*

Both temples are built of white marble, and carved with all the delicacy and richness of ornament which the resources of Indian art of the age in which they were erected could devise.

"Were twenty persons," says Mr. Fergusson,† "asked which of these two temples were the most beautiful, a large majority would, I think, give their vote in favour of the more modern one, which is rich and exuberant in ornament to an extent not easily conceived by one not familiar with the usual forms of Hindu architecture. The difference between the two is much the same that exists between the choir of Westminster Abbey and Henry the Seventh's Chapel that stands behind it. I prefer infinitely the former; but I believe that nine-tenths of those that go over the building prefer the latter."

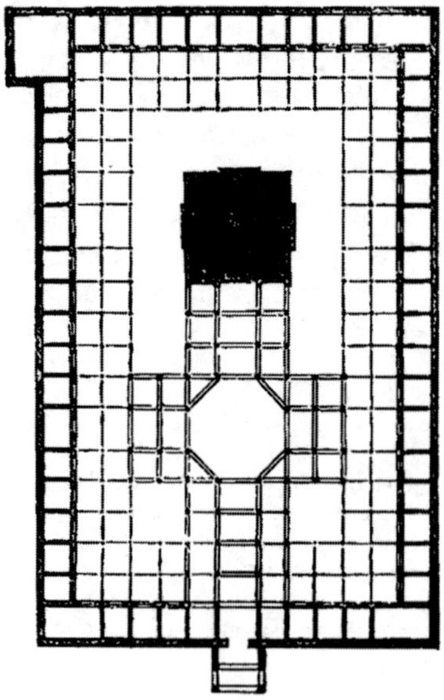

Temple of Vimalasah.—Scale 50 ft. to 1 in.
From Fergusson's *Architecture*, vol. ii. p. 623.

The plan of the temple of Vimalaśah will be easily understood from the annexed woodcut, and it will also suffice to explain the general arrangements of Jaina temples, which, though of very great variety in size,

* *Asiatic Researches*, vol. xvi. p. 312.

† *Picturesque Illustrations of Ancient Architecture in Hindostan*, p. 39.

VII. MOUNT ABU, THE JAIN TEMPLES AT DELWÁDÁ.

are mostly tolerably similar in plan. It consists of a shrine (*c*) lighted only from the door, containing a cross-legged seated figure, in brass, of the first Jina—Adiśvara, to whom this temple is dedicated:—

"Behold the spot,
Where high upraised, with regal ensigns round,
Enthroned sits the BRAZEN DEMIGOD!
Gaze on these lineaments, that awe-ful front,
Meet semblance deemed of the sublimest hope
Vouchsafed to man." *

In front of this is a portico which, with the shrine, is raised five steps above the surrounding court. This is approached through the *mandap*, or outer portico, of twelve columns, arranged in a square covered by a dome resting on eight of these; the two inner columns on each side being so arranged as to form an octagon. The whole is enclosed in an oblong court-yard about 140 feet by 90 feet, surrounded by fifty-five cells, each of which contains a cross-legged statue of one or other of the Tirthankars:—

"High honoured they: in several cell apart,
Each meditative god or mortal sits,
As in devoutest contemplation wrapped."

The door-posts and lintels of these cells or subordinate shrines are carved in most elaborate devices, with human figures interspersed with foliage and architectural ornaments of the most varied complexity. In front of these cells, and forming porticoes to them, is a double colonnade of smaller pillars, their bases standing on a platform raised three steps above the court. In a small cell in the south-west corner is the image of Ambâji, a *devi* or familiar goddess, always associated with Neminâtha,† Chakresvarî being the *Śâsana-devî* of Adiśvara or Rishabha; but as Vastupâla's temple is dedicated to Neminâtha, and the adjoining cell contains also a colossal black marble image of the same Tirthankar, it may possibly be an indication that this temple was also at first dedicated to Neminâtha. On each of the three outer faces of the mandap or dome, the roof is carried over four pillars to that of the corridor in front of the cells, thus leaving two small square courts near the front corners of the enclosure, besides the open space round the central shrine, to admit light to the whole area.

"Externally," says Mr. Fergusson,‡ "the temple is perfectly plain, and there is nothing to indicate the magnificence within except the spire"—or rather pyramidal roof—"of the cell peeping over the plain wall; though even this is the most insignificant part of the erection." And, as he remarks elsewhere, "the external porch, too, is insignificant, so that one is totally unprepared for the splendour of the interior; but I do not know anything in architecture so startling as the effect when the door is opened, and the interior first bursts on the astonished traveller." Indeed it is scarcely an exaggeration to say,—as has already been said of this and its sister temple,—

"'Tis airy lightness all, as if the hand
Of Grecian Artist, in felicitous mood,
Had reared it for the Graces: Elegance
Smiles on the scene, and Beauty's ministers
Are guardians here, and wave their light wings round.
Round thee the polished alabaster sheds
A more than earthly brightness; the white floor
Shows like a sea of milk; the pillars stand
Symmetrical, its fellow answering each,
Alike embossed, alike with quaint device
Endlessly blazoned,—or with bestial shape,
Or human, in each varying attitude
And drapery,—flute, and song, and merry dance
Fantastically blended." §

* *Oriental Chris. Spec.*, ut sup.

† Tod says this cell is dedicated to Bhavânî. (*Travels*, p. 106.)

‡ *History of Architecture* (ed. 1867), vol. ii. p. 265.

§ *Orient. Chris. Spect.*, ut sup., p. 523.

"Outside the temple, and facing the entrance, is a square building, supported by pillars, and containing nine elephantine statues, each of one block of white marble, about four feet in height. On each of them is (or rather was, for the Mogra," or Mughal, "Râja has been at work here), besides the Mahaut, a male figure seated on a rich howdah." They represented the worthy Śeth, or merchant, Vimalaśah, and his family going in procession to the temple. He, however, having been carried off, an equestrian statue of him has been placed in the doorway—"a most painful specimen of modern art, made of stucco, and painted in a style that a sign-painter in England would be ashamed of."

In Vastupâla's temple this procession, with an elaborately carved dahgoba in the centre, "occupies the place of the cells behind the vimana," or shrine, "in that of Vimalaśah, and separated from the court by a pierced screen of open tracery, the only one I know of, of that age; a little rude and heavy, it must be confessed, but still a fine work of its kind. Behind it are ten elephants of very exquisite workmanship, and with rich trappings sculptured with the most exquisite precision. The 'Mogra Râja' has, however, carried off all the riders. In this case, however, the loss is not so great, as behind each elephant is a niche containing statues in alto-relievo of those who were, or were to be, mounted on them. There are Vastupâla, with his one wife; Tejapâla, with two; and their uncle, who seems to have been blessed with three; in short, the whole family party. The men are fine-looking fellows, all with long flowing beards; but I cannot say much for the ladies, who are generally sharp-visaged, sour-looking dames."*

---

* *Picturesque Illustrations*, p. 40; and compare Tod's *Travels*, pp. 107, 108, 111.

VIII. MOUNT ABU, JAIN TEMPLE, INTERIOR.

THE CEILING OF THE DOME.

Photograph IX.

THE temple of Vastupâla and Tejapâla is to the north of Vimala Śah's, and is entered from the court between them by a stair near the west end of the enclosure. It contains several inscriptions in Sanskrit verse, from one of which the following extracts relating to the founders, &c., are taken :—

"I salute the goddess *Śarasvatî*, who pervades the minds of the learned, and is to be attracted only by that intellect in which she takes up her abode. (2) May that *Śiva*, who sees all things in the twinkling of his eye, glowing with the fire of wrath, alone to be appeased by consuming the body of *Kâma*, be propitious to you, together with the son of *Śiva* (*i.e.* Ganéśa).

(3) There is a city named *Anahilla*,* the reservoir of happiness to the people, protected by the *Châlukyas*, equal to *Rughu*, where the moon-like loveliness of the females irradiates the dark half of the lunar revolution, and banishes the gloom of the fortnight. (4) In that city was *Chandapa*, the gem of the *Prâgvâta* race, whose fame was as white as the flower of the jasmin, and by whose liberality the all-bestowing tree of heaven was overcome; the fruit of the maturity of his virtue. (5) His son was *Chandraprasâda*, the golden pillar of the palace of his family, a wide-spreading banner of glory. (6) *Soma* was born from him. . . . . (7) From him was born *Asvarâja*, devoting his mind to undeviating faith in the supreme divinity *Jina;* his beloved queen was *Kamalâ Devî*, like the consort of the enemy of *Tripura*, the mother of *Kumâra*. (8) The first son of these two was named Mantri *Luniga*. . . . . (10) *Śrî Malla Deva*, his next brother, who worshipped *Malladeva*,† was an excellent minister, whose well-governed understanding had no thought of the wealth or wives of others. . . . . (13) The younger brother of this self-restricted sage, the pious VASTUPÂLA, a shower of delight, marvellously laden with the nectar of eloquence, effaces those letters that indicate misfortune on the foreheads of the learned. (14) The chief *Vastupâla* among the ministers and poets of the *Châlukya* race, filches not the property of others, either in fortune or in fancy. (15) *Tejapâla*, the youngest of the whole, is celebrated throughout the universe; the chief of ministers, he shines, augmenting the radiance of his lord, the terror of the wicked. . . . . (17) There were seven sisters of these princes, *Jahtâ*, *Mao*, &c. . . . (19) Whose heart is not delighted by *Vastupâla*, accompanied by his younger brother *Tejapâla*, like the month Madhu by Spring! . . . (22) Long may these brothers enjoy health and life, by whose fame the bracelet of the world is set with pearls, &c. . . . .

(25) "A distinguished scion of the branch of the *Châlukya* heroes was *Arna*, an illustrious prince. (26) After him, with uninterrupted radiance, *Lavanaprasâda*, his enemies being broken, obtained the earth. . . . (27) The son of this prince was *Viradhavala*, (28) who admitted not in his ear the reports of informers affecting these two ministers, by whom the dominion of their lord was irradiated with prosperity, and the courts of the palace were crowded with elephants and steeds. (29) By this couple of ministers placed at his knees I know well that this prince holds prosperity as with his two arms in delightful embrace again.

(30) "This mountain ARBUDA, the peak of clustered hills, is the progeny of the father-in-law‡ of (*Śiva*) the bridegroom of *Gaurî*, the brother-in-law of *Sasibhrit*, who bears the *Mandâkinî* as an ornament in the thick and tangled tresses of his head. . . . . (33) *Dhûma Râja* was the first prince descended from the *Prâmara*. . . . . (34) *Dhunduka*, *Dhruva*, and other princes, were born in this family . . . and at last *Râma Deva*. . . . . (35) His son was *Yasodhavala*, who was not overcome by *Pradyumna;* . . . . who defeated *Valâla*, the king of *Mâlava*, when engaged in hostilities against the Châlukya *Kumâra Pâla*.§ (36) *Dharavarsha* was his son. . . . . (38) His younger brother was *Prahlâdana*, whose sword was sharp in the defence of the sovereign of *Gurjara*, when his power was curbed in the field by *Samanta Sinhâ*. . . . (40) The son of *Dharavarsha* was *Soma Sinha*. . . . . (42) His son was *Krishna Râjadeva*."

It then returns to Vastupâla, and his wife Lalitâ Devî, whose son was Jayanta, or Jaitra Sinha. The genealogy of Anûpamâ Devî, the wife of Tejapâla, follows. Their son was Lâvanya, or Luna Sinha. Malladeva had by Lîlukâ a son Pûrna Sinha, and by Ahlanî Devî was Pethara. It then proceeds,—

(60) "For securing the happiness of his wife and son, *Tejapâla* erected the temple of *Neminâth* on the mountain *Arbuda*. (61) *Tejapâla*, the friend of the king of the earth, erected the temple of *Neminâth* with massive stones, as white as the conch, the jasmin, or the lunar ray; in front of it he constructed a pavilion; by the side of it, fifty-two places for the reception of the chief Jinas; a *batânaka* (?) in the front. (62) The son of *Chandapa* was *Chandraprasâda; Soma* was his son, and his son was *Asavrâja;* his four sons were *Luniga*, *Malladeva*, *Vastupâla*, and *Tejapâla; Jaitra Sinha* was the son of Vastupâla, and *Lâvanya Sinha*, the son of Tejapâla. (63) The figures of these ten riding on female elephants, like the regents of the ten spheres coming to see the *Jina*, are here resplendent.

---

* This is Anahillavâḍâ Paṭṭan, the old capital of Gujarat, to the west of Siddhapur, known to the Arabs of the tenth and following centuries as *Nehrwalah*, on the site of the modern Pâtan or Pirân Pâtan.

† The nineteenth of the twenty-four Jinas or Tirthankaras.

‡ That is *Himâlaya*, from which the Muni or Sage Vasishtha is said to have brought Mount Abu.

§ King of Gujarat, A.D. 1142—1173.

(64) Behind the figures, mounted on elephants, there are also these ten persons, accompanied by their wives, sculptured on a clear stone. The younger brother of *Vastupâla*, the wise Tejapâla, the unequalled friend of the Châlukya Prince *Vira Dhavala*, had these executed. . . . (73) *Śrî Soma Deva*, by whom the feet of the Châlukya monarch are honoured, composed this resplendent panegyric on this holy place. (74) May this eulogium of the race of *Vastupâla* be propitious through the favour of the mother of *Neminâtha*. This eulogy was engraved by the artist *Chandeśvara*, the son of *Dhandhala*, the son of *Kihlana*, and the consecration was performed by *Vijaya Sena Suri*, on the mountain *Arbuda*, on Sunday, the third of the light fortnight of Phâlgun, in the year of Vikrama 1287." (A.D. 1230.)

Over the doors of the cells or Kulikâs there are some forty-six inscriptions recording their construction and grants for the worship of the different images they enshrine, chiefly by Tejapâla or some of his kindred, and dated from Samvat 1287 to 1293 (A.D. 1230 to 1236). These inscriptions fix the date of this Chaitya or temple; and another long one shows that the inhabitants of Chandravatî, at the foot of Abu, had special rights connected with it. The brothers Vastupâla and Tejapâla were Porwâla Vânias of Anahillapaṭṭana, who served as chief ministers under Vîra Dhavala, the first of the Wâghelâ dynasty of Gujarat.*

The *mandap*, or portico, forms one of the distinguishing characteristics of the Jaina style of architecture, as well as its most beautiful feature. In most existing instances it is surmounted by a dome, resting on eight columns out of twelve, which form a square with four columns on each side, including the corners. These pillars terminate in the usual bracket-capital of the East; "upon this an upper dwarf column or attic, if it may be so called, is placed to give them additional height, and on these upper columns rest the great beams or architraves, which support the dome; as, however, the bearing is long, at least in appearance, the weight is relieved by the curious angular strut or truss of white marble, which, springing from the lower capital, seems to support the middle of the beam." The arch formed by the two struts between each pair of columns is known as the *toran*. "That this last feature is derived from some wooden or carpentry original," continues Mr. Fergusson,† "can, I think, scarcely be doubted; but in what manner it was first introduced into masonry construction is unknown. . . . It continues as an architectural feature down almost to the present day, but gradually becoming more and more attenuated, till at last it loses all its constructive significance as a supporting member, and dwindles into a mere ornament."

On the octagon formed by the great marble beams across the heads of the pillars, rests the dome. In this instance a single block in the angles of the octagon suffices to introduce the circle. Above the second row of ornaments, sixteen pedestals are introduced, the lower portions of each wrought into a sitting figure with four or six arms. The pedestals support statues male and female, which, having lately become loose, have been refixed in a very clumsy way with an unnecessary amount of white lime. Above their heads is a circle of twenty-four pendants, and inside this a sort of shell pattern, whilst in the centre is a pendant of the most exquisite beauty.

"The whole is in white marble, and finished with a delicacy of detail and appropriateness of ornament, which is probably unsurpassed by any similar example to be found anywhere else. Those introduced by the Gothic architects in Henry the Seventh's chapel at Westminster, or at Oxford, are coarse and clumsy in comparison."‡

"That fretwork,—that low-pendent ornament,
A faëry maze, voluminous, orb on orb,—
Those waving lines of exquisite tracery,—
Arches of unimaginable sweep,—
Whence every moment on thy charmed eye
New lurking graces laughingly gleam out."

* See the writer's introduction to *The Temples of Śatrunjaya*, p. 12.

† *Hist. Architect.* vol. ii. p. 625.

‡ Fergusson, ut sup.

IX. CEILING OF JAIN TEMPLE.

X. JAIN TEMPLE AT RANPUR.

THE TEMPLE OF RÂNPUR NEAR SÂDRI.

Photographs X. *and* XI.

IN the long and troubled history of Mewar there is perhaps no other reign of greater success than that of Kumbho or Komal Râṇâ, who succeeded his father in A.D. 1418 (Sam. 1475), and ruled with energy for the long period of fifty years. During his reign the country recovered the effects of the invasion of Ala-ud-din Khilji in 1303 He beat back the combined armies of the Muhammadan kings of Gujarat and Malwa in 1440; and soon after, with the aid of Malwa, he defeated the forces of the Dehli emperor at Jhunjunu; and he embellished his dominions by public buildings erected in every corner, but more especially in his capital of Chittur.

Of those consecrated to religion, two, according to Tod, "have survived; that of Kumbho Śyâm, on Abu, which, though worthy to attract notice elsewhere, is here eclipsed by a crowd of more interesting objects. The other, one of the largest edifices existing, cost upwards of a million sterling, towards which Kumbho contributed eighty thousand pounds. It is erected in the Sâdri pass, leading from the western descent of the highlands of Méwar, and is dedicated to Rishabhadeva. Its secluded position has preserved it from bigoted fury, and its only visitants now are the wild beasts, who take shelter in its sanctuary." Tod, however, had never seen the temple, and seems to have had a very imperfect idea of it.* Nor is it yet known as it deserves to be. Mr. Fergusson examined it in 1839, and was perhaps the first European that ever visited this temple, unless it was the late Colonel Spiers, when resident at Sirohi. It is certainly one of the most complete Jaina temples in India, and is well deserving of all that has been said by Fergusson in its praise. Delwâḍâ no doubt excels it both in material and richness of detail, but does not approach it in general effect, and one can only regret that full details and descriptions are not published of such a typical example of a style carried to the highest effect it has ever reached.

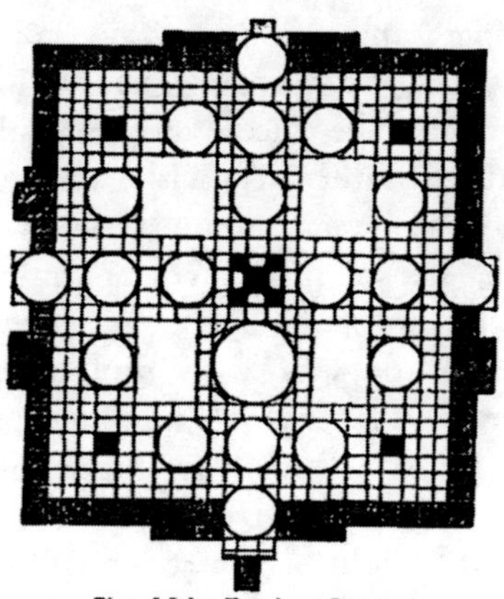

Plan of Jaina Temple at Ranpur.
Scale 100 ft. to 1 in.
From Fergusson's *Architecture*, vol. ii. p. 628.

It is raised on a lofty basement, and, exclusive of the projections on each face, its form is nearly a square, measuring 194 feet 3 inches from north to south, by about 220 feet from east to west; but its

---

* *Annals of Rajasthan*, vol. i. p. 289, or Madras ed. p. 242.

extreme dimensions are about 275 feet by 300. In the centre stands the shrine—a *chaumukh* one, on four sides, and enclosing a quadruple statue of Rishabhanâth, the first of the Tirthankars. Above in the upper story, are similar statues, approached by doors opening on the terraced roofs of the bui On the west door of the principal shrine is an inscription, considerably damaged, and never translated which bears date Samvat 1496—that is A.D. 1439. "The Rânâ's minister,"* says Tod, "of the Jain and of the tribe Porwâr . . . . laid the foundation of this temple in A.D. 1438. It was complete subscription." In front of each door of the shrine is the usual mandap, 20 ft. 1 in. in diameter ins except the one in front of the west or principal entrance, which is a double one, or, a dome of the size as the others inside another 33 feet in diameter, or 38 feet over the columns, which are twel number. The roof is also more richly carved than those of the other three. These domes are on the pla of the shrine, which is raised by five steps above the level of the rest of the floor, on which, at the of the domes, are four open courts; those on the west front measuring 38 feet 3 in. by 21 feet 3 in. those on the east 27 feet 3 inches square. In the north-west court grows the Râyana tree (*Mim hexandria*) sacred to Rishabhanâth, as the Bodhi, or Pipal, is to Buddha, being that under which the he was standing when he attained *moksha*, or beatitude,† and which is a necessary accompaniment o temple, as the Mango is of Neminâth's, the *Chironjia sapida* of Pârśvanâth's, &c. Under the tree is p a tablet, with the *padukâ*, or representation of his feet,—this being considered as symbolical of the spi dominion of the Jina.

In front of each of the four mandaps mentioned above is a lofty dome, 20 feet to 20 feet in diameter inside, and three stories in height, the top of the inner circle of eight pillars being 19 8 in. from the floor, and giving support to the second gallery, the bottom of the parapet or stone of which is 23 feet 1½ in. from the floor, and the top of the pillars in this second gallery beir a height of 28 feet 1 in., while the spring of the dome above the architraves is 29 feet 4 in. Over this rises a beautifully carved dome. "These are," as Mr. Fergusson‡ very justly remarks, principal ornaments of the building. Either, however, they were never completed, or the *torans* or t buttresses, which spring, as at Abu, from the lower capitals, have been removed, only one remainin *situ*. . . . Its presence, however, is sufficient to show what was intended, even if never executed." In corner of the court is a separate shrine, and on each side of the north and south entrances is anc eight in all, and each of these again has its proper mandap to the east or west of it, and beyonc high domes are four more projecting into the faces of the building, "thus making twenty domes foı whole building, all of which are sculptured internally with the most elaborate ornaments, and adorned pendants from their centres, carved with as much minuteness as the nature of the stone will allow; v here, unfortunately, is not white marble, but a rather coarse-grained sandstone, though of crystalline te and good colour. About 420 columns are employed to support these domes with their accompar colonnades, all of which are adorned more or less with sculpture, and no two of which are exactly : but most of them varied to a considerable extent. The internal effect of this forest of columns ma gathered from the view." (Photograph XI.) "But it is impossible that any view can reproduce the en variety of perspective and of light and shade which results from the disposition of the pillars, and o domes, and from the mode in which the light is introduced. A wonderful effect also results from number of cells."§ Besides the five shrines inside the court, there are seventy-six cells || of different f and sizes surrounding the court, and all their façades are more or less adorned with sculpture, while are crowned by the pyramidal *Śikhras* seen over the outer wall.

Under one of the domes is a large figure of an elephant; in a gallery over the south entrance

---

* *Annals of Rajasthan*, ut sup.

† Conf. Hemachaudra, *Abhidâna Chintamaṇi*, 1142 and 1136 (ed. Boehtlingk and Rieu), pp. 213 and 211: Deslongchamps, *Amara* pp. 87—89; *Śatrunjaya Mâhâtmya*, i. 270—279; and the author's Introduction to *The Temples of Śatrunjaya*, p. 21.

‡ *Picturesque Illustrations*, pp. 41, 42.

§ Fergusson, *History of Architecture*, vol. ii. pp. 628, 629.

|| This includes the four shrines on the north and south sides.

XI. JAIN TEMPLE AT RANPUR—INTERIOR.

image with *pâduka* or footmarks; and against the wall stands a large slab, on which is carved a figure of Parśvanâth, the twenty-third Tirthankara, with two female figures as *kausagiya* or supporters, and over his head a canopy of snakes' heads in nine or ten concentric circles, containing not less than 250 heads. Outside the *kausagiya* are two Nâginîs, having the heads and bodies of women, but ending in a snaky coil; these have over their heads the seven-headed snake, so frequent in Buddhist sculptures, and in their inner hands hold each a *chauri*, or fly-flap, on the horizontally held shank of which stands a small figure of an elephant, with rider. Round the whole is a broad band of intricate carving representing sixteen Nâginîs, whose tails are knotted round them into the most intricate maze. What all this may mean, or what connection it may have with Serpent Worship, it may not be easy to say. In the *Śatruñjaya Mâhâtmya*, however, there is a legend about Dharaṇa, the Nâga king, having come to worship Pârśvanâth while he was engaged in his second *kâyotsarga*, or profound meditation, at Śivapuri, in the Kauśâmbaka forest, when he raised his outspread hood (*phaṇa*) over him as an umbrella; * and to this the sculpture on this slab may have some reference.

The general effect of the Rânpur temple can scarcely be judged of from the view given (Photograph X.), taken from the court of a smaller temple just opposite. It is so large and so encompassed by trees that it is difficult to obtain a good photographic view of it. From Mr. Fergusson's account, already quoted, it may not be amiss to extract also the following remarks: "The immense number of parts in the building, and their general smallness, prevents its laying claim to anything like architectural grandeur; but their variety, their beauty of detail—no two pillars in the whole building being exactly alike—the grace with which they are arranged, the tasteful admixture of domes of different heights with flat ceilings, and the mode in which the light is introduced, combine to produce an excellent effect. Indeed, I know of no other building in India of the same class that leaves so pleasing an impression, or affords so many hints for the graceful arrangement of columns in an interior. Besides its merits of design, its dimensions are by no means to be despised; it covers, altogether, about 48,000 square feet, or nearly as much as one of our ordinary mediæval cathedrals, and, taking the basement into account, is nearly of equal bulk; while in amount of labour, and of sculptural decorations, it far surpasses any." †

"As a whole, I look upon this as about the most satisfactory temple I have seen in India. It is true, it is neither so splendid nor so astonishing as those upon Mount Abu; nor does it belong to so pure an age. But there is a completeness in this one that they want; and the whole is in good taste and good keeping. The only building that at the time I could think of to compare with it is the temple at Kanarak; but it is certainly a '*harmonie de contraste*,' as the French say, not '*d'analogie:*' for there it is an exterior, and all the ornament is external; here, the exterior is quite plain, and all the ornament in the interior: there, there are no pillars; here, the whole architectural ordinance consists of pillars and their epistylia: there the sculpture is principally animated representations of men and animals; here it consists almost exclusively of foliage and architectural ornaments of one sort or other. Yet there certainly is a likeness, if not in the form, at least in the spirit of the buildings; they both reach about the same height of art, are productions of the same class of intellect, and utter the same feelings, though in different words. To my mind they are so much alike that I never could think of the one without thinking of the other, though it is not, perhaps, easy to explain to those less familiar with the buildings themselves why this was the case. In the south of India there are halls larger than this temple, and whose roofs are supported by more than twice the number of columns here employed; but, owing to the inartistic mode in which they are arranged, none of them produce anything like the effect here attained. Indeed, there is a play of light and shade in this temple, without either too much glare or too much gloom in any part of it, and a variety and complexity in its design and disposition, without either confusion or extravagance, that render it to my eye one of the most pleasing columnar interiors I know. Look at it from which point you

---

* *Śat. Mâhât.* xiv. 31—35; Introd. to *The Temples of Śatrunjaya*, pp. 6—25; *Indian Antiquary*, vol. ii. p. 139; and compare *Asiat. Transact.* vol. i. pp. 428—436; Bigandet's *Legend of Gaudama*, 2nd ed. p. 99 (1st ed. p. 69); and Hardy's *Buddhism*, p. 182.

† *Hist. of Architecture*, vol. ii. p. 629.

will, you are never perplexed by a labyrinthine confusion you cannot unravel; and the variety of pers[p] and detail that everywhere opens upon you prevents the eye from ever being fatigued in wan[dering] through it." *

To conclude:—

"One potent mind
Hath framed it, and hath bent with wizard skill
Each individual and inferior mind,
To realise a loved ideal Form.
No disproportion wounds thy curious eye;
From multitudinous things one spirit breathes,
And the deep under-note of Harmony
Steals o'er the trancèd ear."†

---

* *Pictur. Illustrations*, p. 42.

† *Orient. Chris. Spec.* ut sup. p. 524.

XII. THE FORTRESS OF KOMALMER.

KOMALMER.

Photograph XII.

A SHORT distance to the north of Sâdri is the small town of Gâneraw, from which a steep and difficult path or pass leads over the Aravalli Hills into Mewar. At the head of this pass is Kailwâḍâ. About four miles north of Ganeraw, however, is Désurî, which gives name to the only really good pass through these hills; at the head of this is Jelwâḍâ, from which Kailwâḍâ may be reached by a ride of twelve miles across very difficult country. From Kailwâḍâ it is only about three miles to the famed fortress of Komalmer, which is distinctly visible from Sâdri and the neighbouring villages, crowning one of the highest peaks of the Aravalli chain, probably over 3,300 feet above the sea.

Like the Rânpur temple down below it, this stronghold owes its origin to Kumbho Rana. "Of eighty-four fortresses for the defence of Mewâr," says Tod,* "thirty-two were erected by Kumbho. Inferior only to Chittur is that stupendous work, called after him Kumbhomér (pronounced *Komalmér*), 'the hill of Kumbho,' from its natural position, and the works he raised, impregnable to a native army. These works were on the site of a more ancient fortress, of which the mountaineers long held possession. Tradition ascribes it to Sampriti Râja,† a Jain prince in the second century, and a descendant of Chandragupta. . . . When Kumbho captured Nagor he brought away the gates, with the statue of the god Hanuman, who gives his name to the gate which he still guards."

"It would be vain to attempt describing the intricacies of approach to this far-famed abode, whose exterior is delineated" in Photograph XII., as seen from the east. "A massive wall, with numerous towers and pierced battlements, encloses a space of some miles' extent below," and which is covered in every direction by ruins of tanks, embankments, houses, and temples—Brahmanical and Jaina, while the castle rises "tier above tier of battlements to the summit, which is crowned by the *Bâdul Mehal*, or 'cloud palace' of the Râṇâs. Thence the eye ranges over the sandy deserts" of Marwar on the west, and over the chaotic mass of mountains to the south and east. "Besides the Arait-pol or barrier thrown across the first narrow ascent, about one mile from Kailwâḍâ, there is a second called the Hâlâ-pol, intermediate to the Hanuman-pol, the exterior gate of the fortress, between which and the summit there are three more, viz. the gate of victory, the sanguinary gate, and that of Râma, besides the last or Chaugan-pol."

This castle is held by a relative of the Râṇâ of Udaypur, and who, "being of the immediate kin of his sovereign, is one of the *babas* or infants of Mewâr, enumerated in the tribe, called Râṇâwât, with the title of 'Maharâja.'" Nowadays, however, he does not seem to keep any state; there is no garrison to speak of, and the castle is in a dirty, tumble-down condition. The view from the summit over the plains of Godwâr is very fine; so also is the wild scenery through which the castle is approached from Kailwâḍâ. Among the many ruins in the large enclosure below the castle are some fine temples, but nothing older than the first half of the fifteenth century. Some of those just below the castle are still used; but one of the largest is a triple temple with a *chauri*, or open hall of three stories, in front of it (part of which appears on the left in the

---

* *Annals of Rajasthan*, vol. i. pp. 288 and 669, 670 (Madras ed. pp. 241, and 575, 576).

† Samprati is said to have been the son of Kuṇâla the Blind, and grandson of Aśoka, who reigned at Pâtaliputra B.C. 263—227. Samprati is said to have reigned at Ujjayin about 200 B.C., and is regarded by the Jains as one of their greatest patrons (*Temples of Śatrunjaya*, p. 20.)

Photograph), which are now used as cattle-sheds. On a rising ground, at a still greater distance from the but still 260 feet below it, is a fine temple, partially ruined, consisting of a shrine and small portico, · veranda of elegant columns round it, over which Tod * goes into ecstasies, calling it the "temple of T in Mewar," and attributing it to his imaginary "*Takshac* architect," and to the age of Sampriti Râja. A at it, by anyone acquainted with the development of Hindu art, would be sufficient to convince him that not belong to an earlier age than the beginning of the sixteenth century; and on the jamb of the door inscription,† proving that the temple never was Jaina, as he asserts, notwithstanding the huge black : linga that almost fills the shrine, but that it was built as a Śaiva temple in A.D. 1514, in the re Sangrâm Râṇâ.

* *Annals of Rajasthan*, vol. i. p. 671 (Madras ed. p. 577).

† *Indian Antiquary*, vol. ii. p. 205.

XIII. MARBLE GHÂT AT RÂJNAGAR.

THE MARBLE GHÂṬ AT RÂJNAGAR.

Photograph XIII.

WITH this noble *bănd* or embankment, and its terraced ghâṭ or descent of marble, there is certainly nothing to compare in Europe, and it is one of the finest things even in India. It is about thirty miles north of Udaypur, and is drawn across a gorge between two hills, through which formerly the Gumti flowed southwards from the outer spurs of the Aravalli Hills, and is formed of an enormous rampart of earth faced on the south or lower side by a plain wall, crowned by small *chhatris*, or canopies of marble. On the north side is the descent or ghâṭ to the lake formed by this dam, built throughout of white marble, and 1,115 feet in length. It runs N.W. by W. and S.E. by E., and above its western end is the fort and palace of Râjnagar,—the modern town being on the southern base of the hill; while at the other end, the bănd is flanked by the Kankrauli hill, once fortified also, and on which, among other remains, are the ruins of a fine old temple. But "when Jeswant Rao Pandit, Sindhia's general, occupied the palace," says Mr. Fergusson,* "Jamshir Khan took possession of this temple, and pulled down the greater part of the building to erect fortifications with the materials; and it is sad, indeed, to see columns and cornices heaped up as a bulwark for the defence of a Marâṭhâ or Pindâri. Even the beautiful spire of the vimana has been partly destroyed, and replaced by a round tower—the keep of this profane citadel. Notwithstanding all this, it is even now a picturesque and, in some respects, a beautiful ruin."

The bănd, like the fort and palace of Râjnagar, was constructed by Râja Singh, who ruled on the throne of Mewar or Udaypur from 1653 till 1680, and forms an artificial lake, called from him RÂJASAMUDRA, said to measure, when full, about twenty miles in circumference. A mile further east, at the town of Kankrauli, the embankment is again resumed, but though probably never finished in the same style, the ghâṭ is there much ruined. A short distance beyond the town it trends away to the north, and there consists simply of a great embankment of earth, faced with terraces of stone, probably intended to be faced also with marble, and the embankment planted with trees.

The ghâṭ consists, first, of a terrace paved with marble, 15 feet 9 inches wide; from this there is a descent of 6 ft. 3 in. by means of nine steps, divided lengthwise into ten divisions, each of about 74 feet in length, separated by piers or bays generally of about 21 feet in width, but two of them 71 ft. 9 in., and a third 58 ft. 2 in. wide, and extending 36 feet outwards. The terrace at the foot of these steps is 4 ft. 7 in. wide; and there is then a second flight of nine steps similarly divided, descending 5 ft. 10 in. to a terrace, which, in the large bays or piers, extends forwards about 90 feet, with a breadth in front of 27 feet, where they are crowned by beautiful pavilions, two of them—those shown in the Photograph—consisting of sixteen columns each, and, to quote again from Mr. Fergusson, "all richly sculptured in different patterns, and altogether with more elegance of form and detail than could well be expected from their age;" the third, however,—the one on the smaller pier, and partly shown in the left of the view,—"has only twelve columns; but more sculpture is lavished on its small dimensions than on either of the others; and it is really a very elegant and fairy-like building."

"The roofs," he continues, "like the pillars, are of white marble, most of the compartments being sculptured with considerable elegance, though, it must be confessed, they are not to be compared with the specimens at Chandravatî" (Jalrapattan) "and Baroli, either for design or execution. This arises partly from the inferiority of the workmen employed on them, but also from the ornaments not being of the same purity of style, but belonging to the class which was introduced in the reign of the great Akbar—a strange jumble of Hindu and

---

* *Pictur. Illustrations*, p. 45.

Muhammadan features, neither being pure nor distinct, but mixed one with another, so as to make up a rich and elaborate, it is true, and often highly picturesque, but which one can with difficulty tolerate, after l familiar with both as they existed in their purity before the reign of that monarch.

"The figure sculpture partakes of the corruption of that age, and certainly is inferior to the architec details, though portions of it are pleasing, and some of the mythological combinations were new to me somewhat startling;" on the roof of the middle canopy are figures with wings and crowns which must have borrowed from some Western source; in the eastern one are dancers in a circle round a central flower, d apsarases, geometric figures, gandharvas with human heads and the bodies and feet of fowls, &c.

Between each pair of piers, and on the same level with the canopies, are two triumphal arches; origi there have been six, but one is entirely gone, one lies a mass of ruin, a third has lost the toran betweer pillars which support the lintel or architrave, and of the most westerly only parts of the pillars are left.

A third descent of 6 ft. 3 in. by nine steps, leads to another terrace, which, however, when the lake is after the rains, is generally covered with water. The next descent is of 6 ft. 4 in., but is accomplishe narrow stairs descending in front of the last terrace—the steps being at right angles to it, and landing narrow terrace that sweeps round the advanced piers in curved lines; again from this there is another des seldom exposed, even in the driest season. The height of the top of the embankment above the water the view was taken was about 33 feet.

On the piers, under the face of the second terrace, are niches, all—except one which contains an ima filled with long inscriptions relating the history of the Râṇâ's family, and the origin and expense of the b Above, also, there lies a well-carved figure of Lakshmî, somewhat defaced: and on the east end of the l is a small temple, apparently of Chandî, while at the other end there is a rest-house.

Ninety-six lakhs of rupees were contributed by the Rânâ, his chiefs, and opulent subjects, for this g work,* of which the material was from the adjacent quarries. "But," adds Tod, "magnificent, costly, and u as it is, it derives its chief beauty from the benevolent motive to which it owes its birth; to alleviate the mis of a starving population, and make their employment conducive to national benefit, during one of those a visitations of Providence, famine and pestilence, with which these states are sometimes afflicted." It wa fact a famine relief work.

It was in Samvat 1717, or A.D. 1660, that this famine took place, and the following extract from *Râja Valâsa*, as given by Tod, is a simple yet terrific record of its effects:—

"The chief of Mewar, deeply meditating on this extreme distress, determined to raise a monument, which the wretched might be supported, and his own name perpetuated. This was seven years in construc and at its commencement and termination all the rites of sacrifice and oblation were observed.

"The Râṇâ went to implore favour at the temple of the '*four-armed;*'† for though Aśâḍ month was c not a drop of rain fell from the heavens; and, in like manner, the months of Ŝâwan and Bhâdun pa away. For want of water the world was in despair, and people went mad with hunger. Things unknown food were eaten. The husband abandoned the wife, the wife the husband—parents sold their children. T increased the evil; it spread far and wide; even the insects died: they had nothing to feed on. Thous of all ages became victims to hunger. Those who procured food to-day, ate twice what nature required. wind was from the west, a pestilential vapour. The constellations were always visible at night, nor was t a cloud in the sky by day, and thunder and lightning were unknown. Such portents filled mankind dread. Rivers, lakes, and fountains were dried up. Men of wealth meted out the portions of food. ministers of religion forgot their duties. There was no longer distinction of caste, and the Ŝudra and Brah were undistinguishable. Strength, wisdom, caste, tribe, all were abandoned, and food alone was the object. *char varan* (four castes) threw away every symbol of separation; all was lost in hunger. Fruits, flowers, e vegetable thing, even trees were stripped of their bark, to appease the cravings of hunger; nay, man ate m Cities were depopulated. The seed of families was lost, the fishes were extinct, and the hope of extinguished."

* Tod, *Annals of Rajasthan*, vol. i. p. 389 (Mad. ed. p. 331).

† Chatturbhuj, a form of Vishnu, a favourite divinity in Mew.

XIV. THE GREAT TEMPLE OF EKLINGAJI.

EKLINGAJI.

Photograph XIV.

THE two great shrines of Udaypur are—Nâthdwârâ, dedicated to Krishṇa or Dwârkaji, twenty-two miles N.N.E. of the capital on the Banâs, and Eklinga, six or eight miles north, dedicated to Mahâdeva, or Śiva, who is the tutelary divinity of the Râjputs. He is commonly worshipped by them under the usual monolithic phallus or *linga*, or as Panchmukhi represented by a bust with four faces round it and one atop. The sacred bull Nandi, on which Śiva is said to ride when he goes abroad, is always attached to the shrines of Iśvara or Śiva, facing the linga, and is often placed outside the temple in a separate mandap.[*] In this temple he is so placed under an open canopy fronting the shrine; he is cast of brass, and of about the natural size, but his side has been penetrated, possibly by some Musalman invader in search of treasure.

The great temple stands nearly in the centre of a large square court, and consists of a mandap of two stories, with an inner shrine, surmounted by a lofty spire. It is built of white marble, and was erected, according to local tradition, by Hamir Singh, who ruled over Méwâr when at the zenith of its power (A.D. 1301—1365), and who is said to have then only restored an older temple built by Bappa about 740 A.D. It is probable, however, that the present temple was built in 1488 A.D., in the time of Raimal. Round the central shrine there are many smaller ones to subordinate divinities, and on the north side is a temple, apparently older than the others, which, from the sculptures on it, has evidently been erected as a Vaishṇava shrine. It appears in the view, to the right of the Great temple.

The Mahârâṇâs of Mewar are the titulary *diwâns* of Eklinga, and when they visit this temple, supersede the high priest in his duties and perform the ceremonies. All grants by these princes also bear at the head the formula—"By the favour of Śrî Eklinga." The origin of this is handed down by tradition thus:—Bappa, the founder of the Mewar dynasty, was of the Gehlot dynasty of Idar, but had fled from his enemies and lived at Nagindra or Nagda, in this vicinity, and ten miles from Udaypur, in the disguise of a herdsman. In this capacity he was suspected of appropriating the milk of a particular cow to his own use. The habitual dryness of the brown cow, when she returned at even, led him to seek to vindicate himself by watching her, and, following her to a narrow dell, he saw her spontaneously pour the stores of her udder amid the shrubs. There, under a thicket, he found Harîta, a hermit, reposing in a state of profound abstraction, and beside him the linga on which the cow had poured out her milk. This was the spot on which the temple of Eklinga now stands. Bappa now visited Harîta daily with milk for himself and offerings of flowers for the divinity, and in return received instructions in the rites of the worship of Śiva and the title of "Diwân of Eklinga," which has been borne ever since by his descendants, whilst the high-priest of the temple traces his spiritual descent through about seventy predecessors to the sage Harîta.

---

* See the author's *Rock-temples of Elephanta*, §§ 15, 16, and 38, and notes; and Tod's *Annals of Rajasthan*, vol. i. pp. 222, 514 (Mad. ed. pp. 145, 143).

† Conf. the Abu inscription, *Asiatic Researches*, vol. xvi. p. 293; see also *Indian Antiquary*, vol. ii. p. 173.

THE BÂGELÂ TALÂO AT EKLINGJI.

Photograph XV.

CLOSE to the village and great temple is an artificial lake called *Indrasâgar*, with a neat bǎnd or dam terraced with steps down to the water. But to the south of the village about a quarter of a mile is a much larger lake, called the *Bâgelâ*, or *Vâgelâ talâo*, formed by a very substantial bǎnd across the north end of the ravine. It contains some small islands, and stretches its arms up into the dells between the hills that enclose it. On the north-east are some gardens belonging to the temple, and the morning view given in Photograph XV. is taken from one of them, looking towards the south. The scene is one of lonely seclusion and beauty, the mist rising in the distant ravines, and the stately palms reflected in the mirror of the glassy lake, enhancing the charms of scenery that in a Western clime would be visited from far and near.

XV. THE BAGELA LAKE AT EKLINGA.

XVI. OLD VAISHNAVA TEMPLES AT EKLINGA.

VAISHNAVA TEMPLES OF SASBAHU.

Photograph. XVI.

THE western shore of the Bâgelâ Talâo is studded with deserted and ruined temples, some of them standing well into the water, and which were there probably long before the lake was formed, at least of its present dimensions. Several of these temples are Jaina, and contain large images of Ajitanâth, some of which bear inscriptions dated about the middle of the fifteenth century.

But the finest is a group of Vaishnava temples, known as Sâsbahu, on a raised platform. On the east side, facing the lake, there has been a handsome approach, still indicated by four massive pillars. Fronting these is a pretty large temple, of the genuine Northern Châlukya style, with very massive columns and heavy *torans.* The porch (shown in Photograph XVI.), and the lattice stone windows on each side of the mandap, are carved in a very elaborate and striking style of art. The interior is a square of about 23 feet, with wide recesses about 4¾ feet deep on all four sides. The roof is supported by four massive pillars with torans, and all the twelve compartments of the ceiling are filled with very neat intricate sculptures. The place, however, has been long desecrated, and has been used as a dwelling until the roof is besmeared with smoke. There is no image in the shrine, nor any inscription to indicate its age; there are at the entrance only a few names of visitors, with dates varying from the middle of the seventeenth to the beginning of the eighteenth century. But the temple and all the others on the same platform are evidently much older, probably dating from about A.D. 1300, if not from a still earlier age.

One of the smaller shrines is shown on the right of the picture, and behind the larger, and to the north of it, is another, nearly as large, the mandap of which, except on the west, towards the shrine, is open all round, from the top of a low screen wall to the lintels which support the roof. The upper portions of the columns are round, and, together with the screen, are all elaborately carved in a bold clear style, and are in good preservation.

UDAYPUR—THE WATER PALACE.

Photograph XVII.

WHEN Chittor fell to the arms of Akbar in 1568, the Râṇâ Uday Singh fled to Râjpipli, but soon returned to the valley known as the 'Girwâ' or 'Circle,' formed by a spur of the great Araballi range encircling an area of about thirty square miles, watered by the river Berach, which escapes from it by a narrow pass where he had some years previously built a lofty dam, forming, as a defence work, an extensive lake called after him Uday Sâgar. This Girwa is surrounded on all sides by hills rugged and picturesque, through which there is only one pass, a fortified gorge, towards Nimach, by which a wheeled conveyance can pass. About four miles south of the steep ghâṭ, leading from Eklinga, he threw a dam across a mountain torrent, and formed the Pîcholā lake, of considerable extent; and in 1569, on the rising ground beside it, he raised the small palace called Nochoki, around which was soon built his new capital, called after his own name Udaypur.

When full, the Pîcholā lake, "submerging the bǎnds of two others, throws out deep bays into the suburbs; a picturesque bridge unites one of these to the city, and the sparkling water on either side is edged with numerous ghâṭs, gay balconies and temples, shaded with dark foliage. The bold expanse of the lake stretches away beyond from under the lofty palace, and the low yet extensive islands, fringed with marble piazzas, enclosing luxuriant orange gardens interspersed with sombre cypresses, towering palms" and temple spires "shooting up here and there, the whole resting on a background of the dark and lofty Araballi, forms a scene unsurpassed by any other in India. The palace itself is an extensive and imposing pile, but on nearer approach is found to consist of insignificant enclosures, joined by narrow dark passages, and a handsome triple-gated entrance."*

In the lake, on the west, are two islands, containing about four acres apiece; in the more southerly is the Jagnewâs palace, built by Jǎgǎt Singh (A.D. 1627—1653), and in the other is the Jagmandir, partly built by the same Râṇâ. This latter (shown in the photograph) is described with some exaggeration by Tod.† It is divided into three gardens, the end ones nearly square. "Each garden," says Fergusson,‡ "is surrounded by an arcaded cloister, open on both sides, where it merely divides one garden, or court, from the other; but on those sides which are next the water, the arches are filled with stone trellis-work, sometimes flower of patterns of great intricacy, but oftener of geometric forms, most of the openings being filled with stained glass, forming diaper and mosaic patterns. The centre division of each of those sides which stand in the water is occupied by a hall, the arches of which are open towards the garden. Two of these, two stories high, are on the side towards the palace (the one seen in the view); but the principal halls are those at the north and south ends. The former is a splendid apartment of white marble, a square with twelve pillars in the centre and a deep veranda all round. The one at the opposite end is also very handsome. . . . The west side is occupied by" (what were) "the private apartments of the harem, and, though forming the principal bulk of the building, they are not remarkable as architectural objects."

---

* Brooke's *History of Meywar* (Calcutta, 1859), p. 6.

† *Annals of Rajasthan*, vol. i. p. 373 (Madras ed. p. 315); and conf. Forbes, *Ras Mala*, vol. i. p. 403.

‡ *Picturesque Illustrations*, p. 51.

XVII. UDAYPUR—THE WATER-PALACE.

The gardens are laid out in the usual formal style of Indian gardens, but are overcrowded with trees and plants, and the water channels and ornamental details are without taste or art.

The palace of Jagnewâs was the asylum of Khuram, the second son of Jehangir, who had allied himself with Bhim Singh, the brother of the Râṇâ Karna, in a revolt against his father, but was defeated, and found refuge here, where he remained until he came to the throne of Dehli as Shah Jehan, A.D. 1628. With its palace and gardens this island is even finer than the Jagmandir.

These water-palaces have now an additional interest in the eyes of Englishmen as having been the retreat of several of our countrymen and countrywomen during the horrors of the Mutiny of 1857.

"The only objects in Europe," adds Mr. Fergusson, "that can be compared with these are the Borromean islands in the Lago Maggiore, but I need scarcely say their Indian rivals lose nothing by the comparison—they are as superior to them as the Duomo at Milan is to Buckingham Palace. Indeed, I know of nothing that will bear comparison with them anywhere."

MAUSOLEUM OF SANGRAM SINGH.

Photograph XVIII.

ABOUT two miles from Udaypur is the Mahâsatî, or necropolis of the royal family of Mewar, where are th cenotaphs of the Mahârâṇâs, their families, and relations, of the last three hundred years. It is a beautif spot, well shaded by magnificent trees, and crowded with marble monuments, but associated with melanchol feelings as "the scene of the *Satîs*—those sad exhibitions of pride and superstition which have for so lon a period been enacted by the females of this family,"* for the Râṇâs of Udaypur still assert, as a right of their to have their wives burnt with their dead bodies. The necropolis is divided into two parts by a wall: in the or are the large cenotaphs of Amra Singh (A.D. 1596—1620), Karna Singh (A.D 1620—1627), and Jagat Singh (1627-1653), with many smaller ones of members of the royal family, and of others. Some of these are evidently bui of fragments of older buildings; and in this portion there is a very old well or kuṇḍ, with the remains of a sma shrine in the middle of it, ascribed to Gandrufsen, whose name is also associated with coins occasionally foun in the mounds just outside the enclosure, and which mark the site of the ancient city of Ahar—a plac associated with the early history of the Udaypur royal family, as the descendants of Bappa, on their migratic to Nagindra, are said, in the place of Gehlot, to have taken the name Ahârya from it,—a name still borne b the Dungarpur family, founded by the elder branch of the Mewar family about A.D. 1195.†

The other portion of the enclosure contains, besides the commencement of a large tomb for Râjasingh—wh formed the Râjnagar bănd, but who died before completing his own monument in 1680,—two large cenotaphs Amra Singh II. (A.D. 1699—1715) and of Sangrâm Singh II. (A.D. 1715—1733), and smaller ones of their successors A small square platform outside the stylobate of Râjasingh's, marks the spot where his body was burnt wi two of his wives; and with Amra Singh twelve women appear to have been sacrificed.

The view in the Photograph is of Sangrâm Singh's. In front of it is a low brick enclosure, where was bur the body of Râja Singh II. in 1761, with thirteen wives and concubines; and to the right of it is a sma tomb—that of Râṇâ Sărdâr Singh, who died in 1842.

The monument of Sangrâm Singh has never been quite finished. It fronts, and is nearly the counterpa in form and dimensions of Amra Singh's. It stands on a lofty platform, or podium, to which the ascent made by twenty-five steps in three short flights. This platform measures 69 or 70 feet over all, and suppor a chattri, or canopy, the base of which measures 46½ feet square, exclusive of the porches which project each side. The columns of the dome and porches are thirty-six; first the central octagon is increased to square by the introduction of a column at each angle; then four columns are added to each face, formir re-entrant angles at the corners; and lastly two pillars are advanced on each side for the porches.

---

* Brookes, *Hist. of Meywar*, p. 9.

† Tod, *Annals*, vol. i. pp. 260, 793 (Madras ed. pp. 218, 677, 678); Brookes, *Hist. of Meywar*, p. 9.

‡ Near these is the cenotaph of Krishṇâ Kuvârbâî, the daughter of Bhim Singh, whose tragic death is so well known. See Tc *Annals*, vol. i. pp. 461—466 (Madras ed. pp. 395—399).

XVIII. UDAYPUR—CENOTAPH OF SANGRÂM. SINGH.

XIX. CHITTUR—THE JAIN TOWER.

THE KHAITAN STHAMBA AT CHITTUR.

Photograph XIX.

SIXTY-FIVE miles east of Udaypur is Chittur, the old capital of Mewar, wrested from its Mori chief by Bappa in the eighth century, and held by his successors as the stronghold and key of the country till the middle of the sixteenth. There are perhaps few places of greater historical and antiquarian interest in India. It was built on a flat table mountain, conspicuous for its light-coloured scarped rock, springing from a dark-wooded base. The length of the hill is three and a quarter miles, and its breadth, at the widest, is about three-fourths of a mile, but at the end which lies to the S.S.W. it is not more than four hundred yards. "Its height varies from 400 to 500 feet above the plain, of which the last eighty is a natural scarp. The approach is by a zig-zag road from the modern town, built at the foot of the western face of the hill, and which leads through seven gateways to the summit."* The top is covered with the ruins of temples and reservoirs, the *débris* of houses overgrown with custard apple and other shrubs, and interspersed with the huts of a small wretched village.

The tower represented in Photograph XIX. is perhaps the oldest monument of the kind now existing in India. Of its origin we know nothing: one local tradition ascribes it to "Khatan Rani, the wife of Kheta Râṇâ," but of these personages history is entirely silent; another legend ascribes it to Allâta, a descendant of Bappa, and who probably reigned about A.D. 900.† Tod calls it the Khowasin-sthamba, and says he found a fragment of an inscription at its base, reading: "By Śrî Adinâtha, and the twenty-four Jineśvara, Pundarîka, Gaṇeśa, Sûrya, and the nine planets, may you be preserved! Sam. 952 (A.D. 895) Baiśakh (*sudi*) the 30th, Guruvâr (*Thursday*)." Unfortunately, the stone on which Mr. Fergusson found "a long inscription" in 1839, is no longer to be seen: like so many more, it has been carried off by some meddling amateur and lost. That the tower, however, belongs to the end of the tenth century there can be no doubt, nor that it was erected by Jains. It stands on a square pedestal 19 ft. 11 in. square and 9 ft. high, with stairs on the south side; from the top of this a few steps lead up 6 ft. 2 in. to the door. It now commences from a base about 12 ft. 10 in. square outside and 5 ft. 2 in. inside, and ascends by a winding stair through four stories—the fourth floor being 57 ft. 4 in. from the ground; 6 ft. 10 in. above this is the open canopy at the top, the pillars of which are 6 ft. high; and the total height may thus be quite 75 feet. The north side of this canopy with two of the twelve pillars at the top has fallen off, but its extreme dimensions were 15 ft. 4 in. each way. "Altogether," says Mr. Fergusson,‡ "the appearance of this tower is singularly graceful and elegant, . . . but its chief charm, at least to me, lay in the extreme elegance of its mouldings, and the careful and elaborate finish of its details, which are only found in the architecture of its age, or earlier: of these, so few specimens remain in India, that they are, perhaps, the more enjoyed by the antiquary when he does stumble upon them."

A belt about the middle of it is covered with six rows of little figures of *Jinas* or *Tirthankars*, numbering in all upwards of four hundred, and below this, on each face, is a large standing figure of a Jina in a recess or niche.

---

* Brookes, *Meywar*, p. 5; Tod, *Annals*, vol. ii. pp. 755—764 (Madras ed. pp. 691—700).

† Compare Tod, *Annals*, vol. ii. p. 763 (Mad. ed. pp. 698, 699), vol. i. pp. 243, 802 (Mad. ed. pp. 203, 706); Prinsep, *Useful Tables* (ed. Thomas), p. 256; *Asiat. Res.* vol. xvi. pp. 294, 302; and Fergusson's *Pict. Illust.* p. 38.

‡ *Pict. Illustrations*, p. 38.

PALACE OF BHIM AND PADMANI AT CHITTUR.

Photograph XX.

THE remains represented in this Photograph (XX.) are considerably to the south of most of the ot ruins of Chittur, and, from the number of fowl that frequent the lake in which the small pal is situated, they are evidently little visited. They belong to about the thirteenth century, but h undergone some modifications at a later date.

They are interesting, as almost the only relics of the kind left of old Chittur—which was sacked destroyed by Ala-ud-din in 1303. Lakshman Singh succeeded to the throne of Mewar in 1274, and his un Bhimsingh was protector during his minority. Bhim espoused the daughter of Hamir Sank, who was remarkable for her beauty and accomplishments as to receive the title of *Padmanî*—a term bestowed only u the superlatively fair. To obtain possession of her, the Hindu bards allege, Ala-ud-din laid siege to Chitt After a brave defence,* when it was found no longer tenable, that horrible rite the *Johar* was perform The Rajputnîs, the wives and daughters of the defenders, to the number of several thousands, entered in p cession the subterranean chambers of the fort; the fair Padmanî closed the throng, which was augmented whatever of female beauty or youth could be tainted by Tatar lust; and then they were shut in, to fi security from dishonour in the pyre that was lit to devour or suffocate them. The Râṇâ now "calling arou him his devoted clans, for whom life had no longer any charms," dressed in saffron robes, "they threw op the portals and descended to the plain, and with a reckless despair carried death, or met it, in the crowd ranks of Ala. The Tatar conqueror took possession of an inanimate capital, strewed with brave defenders, smoke yet issuing from the recesses where lay consumed the once fair object of his desire; and since t devoted day the cavern has been sacred."† It is on the north side of a tank on the west scarp of the hill.

This is the traditional palace of Bhimsî and his fair but unfortunate Padmanî.

---

* See a glowing account of it in Tod's *Rajasthan*, vol. i. pp. 262—266 (Mad. ed. pp. 220—223).

† Tod, *Annals*, ut sup.

XX. CHITTUR—PALACE OF BHIM AND PADMANI.

XXI. CHITTUR—KOMAL'S KIRTI-STHAMBA.

KUMBHA RANA'S KIRTI STHAMBA.

Photograph XXI.

A KIRTI STHAMBA, or Jaya Sthamba, is a pillar or tower of fame or victory; and this beautiful tower is commemorative of the triumph gained by Kumbhakarṇa in 1439, when, at the head of a hundred thousand horse and foot and fourteen hundred elephants, he defeated the united forces of the Sultans of Malwa and Gujarat, carrying Mahmud, the Ghilji sovereign of Malwa, a prisoner to Chittur. About ten years after this he laid the foundation of this column, which was completed in ten more. It is about 122 feet in height, the base being about 10 feet high and 47 feet square: on this stands the tower, about 30 feet over all; inside which is another hollow tower 11 ft. 6 in. square outside and 5 feet square within. The outer tower is 16 ft. 3 in. square inside, with recesses 7 ft. 1 in. by 4 ft. 10 in. on each face. The stair ascends in alternate stories outside; and within the inner tower, and after ascending 94 ft. 9 in. we reach a chamber 16¼ feet square, the walls filled with open carved work. By a ladder from this we reach the octagonal pavilion, which carries the cupola at the top.

In this chamber there were inscriptions, but two of the four marble slabs on which they were have been carried off, and of the other two only portions have been read. Thus, *śloka* 172 reads: "Shaking the earth, the lords of Gujarkhand (*Gujarat*) and Malwa, both the sultans with armies overwhelming as the ocean, invaded Mîdpât (*Mewar*). Kumbhakarṇa reflected lustre on the land: to what point can we exalt his renown? In the midst of the armies of his foe, Kumbha was as a tiger, or as a flame in a dry forest. . . . *śl.* 183: While the sun continues to warm the earth, may the fame of Kumbha Râṇâ endure. While the icy (Himâlaya) mountains of the north rest upon their bases, while ocean continues to form a garland round earth's neck, so long may Kumbha's glory be perpetuated! May the varied history of his sway last for ever! Seven years had elapsed beyond fifteen hundred (Sam. 1507 or A.D. 1450) when Râṇâ Kumbha placed this ringlet on the forehead of Chittur. Sparkling like the rays of the rising sun, is the *toran*, rising like the bridegroom of the land. In S. 1515 (A.D. 1458) . . . this *Kirti Sthamba* was finished.

The inner wall of the staircase is one mass of mythological sculptures, and has some inscriptions dated A.D. 1448.

"From almost every point where it can be seen," says Mr. Fergusson, "it gains considerably from being placed on the very brink of a precipice, which adds considerably to its apparent height, and gives it a dignity it would not possess if situated on a plain. As a tower its outline is certainly very pleasing, perhaps more so than that of the Khawasin Sthamba, . . . but their details and general execution will not bear comparison, and on the spot there are few, I am convinced, but would agree with me in preferring the older example. Not that the details of this one are bad; indeed, for its age, they are wonderfully well and carefully executed: and certainly no pains have been spared to make them as perfect as possible, the whole tower, from the basement to the summit, being covered with the most elaborate ornament, either in figures or architectural scrolls and foliage; all, however, kept in perfect subordination to the general design, and in perfect keeping as a whole."*

* *Picturesque Illustrations*, p. 43; and see Tod's *Annals*, vol. i. pp. 287, 288, vol. ii. pp. 761, 762 (Mad. ed. vol. i. p. 241, vol. ii. pp. 696, 697).

TEMPLES AND COLUMN AT BAROLI.

Photograph XXII.

ON the south bank of the Chambal and nearly opposite to Bhainsrorgaḍh are the temples of one of the most beautiful groups of Hindu fanes of their age in India. "The effect of their arch is, however," as Mr. Fergusson remarks, "a good deal heightened by the beauty of the scene in they are situated; perhaps, also, by its solitary loneliness, for there is not a tent or house on the plain in which they are situated, nor any sign of human habitation except the little hill fort of Bh perched on a crag overhanging the Chambal, but on the other side of the river, and at a consi distance from the temples. In another direction, at a distance of about two miles, the Chambal through the barrier of the antrea" (or long valley stretching up from Mokandarâ) "in a fall, a beauty, which in the rains must be as fine as those of the Rhine at Schaffhausen, and even when them, in the dry season, were finer than those of the Clyde at Lanark. Like every other scene o than usual beauty and every phenomenon of nature in India, innumerable legends of gods and demigo located around them; and it is probably to one of these that Baroli owes its sanctity and fame, for hear of no town, nor even a tradition of one, having existed in this neighbourhood."

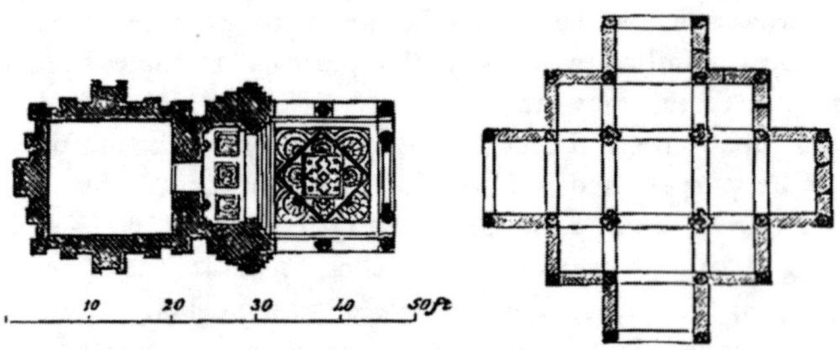

Plan of the larger Temple at Baroli. From Mr. Fergusson's Plan,—*Architecture*, vol. ii. p. 595.

The principal temple here, a little to the right (or north) of the two small ones shown in th probably dates from the latter half of the ninth century. It has long been desecrated, but was originally d to Śiva or Mahâdeva as Rori-Baroli, symbolized by a round waterworn stone laid in a groove in the ring of the Yoni, and so poised that it can be made to revolve, while the votary repeats a *ma* some length.

The style of the architecture does not, at first sight, differ from that of the small ones to th of it. The base of the shrine is plain, with only a niche on each of the three exposed sides, co sculptures of great merit, fully described by Tod. Above the *antarala* or vestibule of the shrine, richly sculptured roof rises to more than two-thirds of the śikhar or spire; and in front of this, again open manḍap or portico, the roof of which "is sculptured with a richness and complexity of design unrivalled even in those days of patient prodigality of labour. The temple, however, is but a sm and the neatly carved spire, with its urn-like *kalas* or finial, only rises to a height of fifty-eight feet, as has been well remarked, "its merit consists entirely in its shape and proportions, and in the elega profusion of the ornament that covers it." "Internally, the roof is far more elaborate and richly carv

XXII. TEMPLES AND COLUMN AT BAROLI.

the exterior. It consists of a square within the entablature, of about 12 ft. 6 in., the corners of which are cut off by four slabs, so as to reduce it to a square of about 9 feet, placed diagonally to the other. This operation is again repeated, and the square becomes a little less than one-half the original one, or about 6 feet, and this opening is closed by one slab, pierced with a quatrefoil trefoiled—to borrow a term from Gothic architecture,—the whole depth of the roof being, by estimation, about 3 feet. It is one of the most elaborate as well as most beautiful specimens of the Hindu mode of roofing to be met with anywhere."

In front of the mandap, and separated from it by four or five yards' distance, is a hall called *Sengâr-Châwaḍî*, or ornamental hall, similar to that in front of the temple at Mudherâ in Gujarat, and one of the finest examples of its kind. It is a square of sixteen columns—four on each face—with four entrances, each with its advanced pair of columns. Each compartment of the roof is covered in on the same principle as that employed for the roof of the mandap, but without the same richness and depth of carving. The centre of the Châwaḍi is the traditional scene of the nuptials of a "Râja Hun with the fair daughter of a Râjput prince, of whom he had long been enamoured," and to commemorate which event these magnificent structures were raised. But of this Râja Hun we know nothing more.

The temple on the right of the view is one dedicated to Pârvatî, the *śaktî* or wife of Śiva. Its śikhar is slightly more spirelike than that of the great temple; it is, however, doubtless of the same age. Beside it is another still smaller; and there are others belonging to the group: one dedicated to Ganeśa; another containing a figure of the *trimurti*, or trifrontal representation of Mahâdeva so common about the ninth century; and another shrine, near the kuṇḍ or sacred fountain, contains a figure of Vishnu reposing on the Śesha Nâga, a beautiful piece of Hindu sculpture.

Nearly in front of the temple of Pârvatî stood two pillars, one of them still erect, and which probably supported an architrave and ornamental pediment, like that at Siddhapur, or in the court of the temple of Achaleśvar at Abu, from which hung a swing for the recreation of the god, as this is a favourite amusement with many of the Hindu gods. This pillar Tod describes, as excelling everything else here.* Four elegant female figures surround the base and form the principal ornament of the shaft. But it has lost its bracket capital, "which is the invariable accompaniment of Indian pillars of every age and style, and is, after all, the most elegant and appropriate mode of supporting an architrave that has yet been invented by the ingenuity of man."

---

* See Fergusson, *Picturesque Illustrations*, pp. 35, 36, and *Hist. of Architecture*, vol. ii. pp. 594, 595, 598; Tod's *Annals of Rajasthan*, vol. ii. pp. 457, 704—713 (Madras ed. pp. 422, 646—653); and conf. *Indian Antiquary*, vol. ii. p. 215; and the author's *Notes of a Visit to Gujarat*, pp. 104—106.

TOMB OF UMED SINGH AT KOTÂ.

Photograph XXIII.

THE small state of Kotâ, in Harautî, at present containing 4,339 square miles, lies to the south-eas the River Chambal and east of Mewar. It was formerly a fief of Bundî, but was presented by Jehangi Madhu Singh, the second son of Rao Ratna, then ruler of Bundi, in reward for his valour at the battl Burhânpur in 1579. In 1770 Rao Goman Singh died, leaving his son and heir Umed Singh, then only years old, in charge of the hereditary faujdâr and commander-in-chief, named Zalim Singh, as regent. Zalim Si was a man of extraordinary ability, and attained a commanding ascendancy over all the Rajpût states. attaining his majority, Umed Singh continued Zalim Singh in the exercise of uncontrolled authority, retair only the outward show of sovereignty, which was scrupulously conceded to him by his able regent. This s of affairs continued till the death of Umed Singh in November, 1819. It is the mausoleum of this prince appears in the view. It is of considerable size and pretensions, and the taste displayed in its style and arrar ment is good considering the age to which it belongs; the dome, however, appears heavy for its suppor pillars, and the style is much more Muhammadan than Hindu.*

---

* See Tod's *Annals*, vol. ii. pp. 505—559, 662—665, 727, 740, and 773 (Madras ed. vol. ii. pp. 466—514, 607—610, 665, 666, 677, and 7 Thornton, *Mem. of War in India*, pp. 357—360; Malcolm, *Central India*, vol. i. p. 504, vol. ii. p. 500; Elphinstone, *Hist. of India*, vol. ii. pp. 521; Duff, *Hist. of the Mahrattas*, vol. iii. p. 280; Aitcheson's *Collection of Treaties*, vol. iv. pp. 71 *seqq.*; &c.

XXIII. CENOTAPH OF UMED SINGH AT KOTA.

XXIV. STREET VIEW AND PALACE AT BUNDI.

STREET VIEW AND PALACE AT BUNDI.

Photograph XXIV.

TWENTY-TWO miles north-west of Kotâ lies Bundi, the capital of the Rajput state of the same name. It is said to have been founded in 1341 by Rao Deva, a Hârâ Râjput, who took the Bandu valley from the aboriginal Minas who possessed it, ruthlessly slaughtering its rude inhabitants. It is picturesquely situated in a small valley or basin nearly surrounded by rocky hills, and has a fine hill-fort. The hill of the fort is about two miles long and one in breadth, with very pretty valleys on its north and south sides, each with its small stream, across which bănds are thrown to form two artificial lakes, between which the town is situated. The northern one is about a mile and a half long, and at the upper end of it are the *Mahâsatîs* or cenotaphs of the Royal family of Bundi.

The principal bazaar is a very picturesque street, and leads directly to the palace gate. The view embraces a part of this street and a portion of the palace, but the latter is better seen from other points, whence it appears lying higher up on the hill. The whole building, says Tod, "is an aggregate of palaces, each having the name of its founder; and yet the whole so well harmonizes, and the character of the architecture is so uniform, that its breaks or fantasies appear only to arise from the peculiarity of the position, and serve to diversify its beauties. The Chattrmehal, or that built by Râja Chattra Sâl (1652—1658), is the most extensive and most modern addition. It has two noble halls, supported by double ranges of columns of serpentine." Mr. Fergusson characterises it as "a fine specimen of an Indian palace, and though it aims at no architectural display, and is merely an aggregation of different buildings grouped together, without the smallest attempt at regularity or effect, it produces a far more pleasing combination of forms than usually arises from more studied designs; and when seen at a little distance, lying on the side of a hill rising from its lakes, and crowned by the hill-fort, it is as pleasing a piece of architectural scenery as I have seen anywhere, even in India, where such effects are common."*

---

* Consult Tod's *Annals*, vol. ii. pp. 460—504, 692—699 (Madras ed. vol. ii. pp. 424—465, 634—641); Fergusson's *Pict. Illust.* p. 53; *Jour. Asiat. Soc. Beng.* vol. ii. (1833), p. 400; Broughton's *Letters from a Mahratta Camp*, p. 165; Duff's *Hist. of the Mahrattas*, vol. iii. pp. 267, 311; Sutherland's *Sketches of the Relations between the British and the Native States* (2nd ed. Calcutta, 1837), pp. 87—97; Capt. Burton's *Narr. of the Boondee Principality*; *Asiat. Resear.* vol. vi. p. 66; Briggs' *Ferishta*, vol. ii. p. 233; &c.

AJMER.

Photograph XXV.

AJMER is the capital of the British districts in Rajputana, and is beautifully situated on the north-eastern s of a hill—one of a number which surrounds the basin or small valley in which it stands. It is surrounde a wall of stone, and has five gateways—all on the north and west sides. The houses of the wealthier cla are well built, and the principal streets are wide and handsome. Above the city, on the crest of the hi the west, at the base of which it stands, is the old fort of Târâgarh, where are the residences of some of officials. There are also some pretty villas on the *band* of the Ana-sagar, a beautiful artificial lake to the n of the town, which sometimes attains a circumference of six miles in the rainy season, and is said to owe its origi Ana or Anal Raja, who reigned here about the end of the eleventh or beginning of the twelfth century. Abc mile to the east, in the centre of the valley, is another artificial lake, the Bîsal-talâo—from Bisal, or Vîra E the grandfather of Anâ, who formed it about the middle of the eleventh century. It is an oval, two an half miles in circumference and originally faced all round with stone.

Near the former of these is the "Daulat Bagh," or "garden of wealth," built by Jehangir for his resid when he undertook to conquer the Râjputs. This is the palace in which he received the English Ambass sent by James I.

About eight miles west of Ajmer is the sacred lake and town of Pushkar or Brahma-kâ Sthân at the of the Ajaypâl hills.*

---

* See *Indian Antiquary*, vol. i. p. 275; Tod's *Annals*, vol. i. pp. 777—784 (Madras ed. 664—670); Cunningham's *Archæolog. Surv. Rep.* v pp. 252 *seqq.*; Jacquemont, *Voyages*, tom. vi. pp. 389—391; Irvine's *General and Medical Topography of Ajmere*, pp. 42—47, 58—68, 95, 97, 112, Briggs' *Ferishta*, vol. i. pp. 47, 172, 173, 177, vol. ii. p. 208; Fraser's *Journey from Delhi to Bombay;* Bird's *Mirat-i Ahmadi*, pp. 24, 25, 71, 72 Boileau's *Personal Narrative*, p. 150 *seq.*; Heber's *Journal*, vol. ii. (12mo. ed.), pp. 48 *seqq.*; &c.

XXV. AJMER, FROM ABOVE THE 'DAULAT BAGH.'

XXVI. AJMER, THE ARHAI-DIN-KA JHOPRA.

THE ARHAI-DIN-KA JHOPRA, AJMER.

Photograph XXVI.

AJMER "has been too long the haunt of Mughuls and Pathans, the Goths and Vandals of Rajasthan," says Tod, to afford much scope to the researches of the antiquary. Whatever time had spared of the hallowed relics of old, bigotry has destroyed, or raised to herself altars of materials, whose sculptured fragments serve now as disjointed memorials of two distinct and distant eras: that of the independent Hindu, and that of the conquering Muhammadan, whose 'Idgahs and mosks, mausoleums and country-seats, constructed from the wrecks of aboriginal art, are fast mouldering to decay." Nor are these reflections uncalled for, or too strongly expressed; no vestige perhaps remains of the Ajmer that was taken by Muhammad Ghori in 1193; nor are the Muhammadans anywhere more superstitiously bigoted and insolent than under British rule in Ajmer. Fortunately, the only place worth visiting is no longer used, and consequently is not looked upon by them, equally with the idol-worshipping Hindus, as desecrated by the presence of shoe-leather.

On the declivity of Târâgaḍh, and just on the outskirts of the city, are the ruins of the *Arhai-din-ka jhopra*, or "shed of two and a half days,"—a name indicative of the astonishing rapidity with which it was erected. Tod supposes this splendid ruin to have been a Jaina erection, to which the Muhammadans only added the great screen to convert it into a mosk. A little attention, however, will convince the visitor, that, like the remains at the Kutb Minar near Delhi, the entire design and arrangement are Muslim but the columns and roofs are the spoils of Hindu or Jaina temples, thrown down by the conqueror, and the materials used to raise this once magnificent temple to the self-exalting creed of Islâm. In his perplexity as to the origin of such a pile, Tod appropriately quotes the lines:—

> "I asked of *Time* for whom *those* temples rose,
> That prostrate by his hand in silence lie:
> His lips disdained the myst'ry to disclose,
> And, borne on swifter wing, he hurried by!
> The broken columns *whose?* I asked of *Fame;*
> (Her kindling breath gives life to works sublime;)
> With downcast looks of mingled grief and shame,
> She heaved the uncertain sigh, and followed Time.
> Wrapt in amazement, o'er the mouldering pile
> I saw *Oblivion* pass with giant stride;
> And while his visage wore Pride's scornful smile,
> 'Haply *thou know'st*, then tell me, *whose*,' I cried,
> '*Whose* these vast domes that ev'n in ruins shine?'
> 'I reck not whose,' he said, 'they now are mine.'"

This masjid, like many others elsewhere, is in an enclosure 260 ft. by 248 ft. with towers at the corners, and surrounded on the north, west, and south sides by cloisters, raised on Hindu pillars, but now almost entirely ruined. The principal entrance is on the east side, but there is another with a projecting porch on the south—the north side being built against the scarped rock of the hill. In the west side of this enclosure is the mosk—or rather what remains of it, about 200 ft. long by 41 ft. wide, supported by five rows of lofty pillars, including the row let into the back wall,—over 120 in all,—and each formed of two Hindu columns. The front row excepted, the remaining four rows support seven octagonal recessed roofs—domes they cannot be called:

the front row of columns carries the cloister roofs which fill up the space to the front wall. In front ‹ is a screen wall 11½ ft. thick, and 56 ft. high, pierced with seven pointed arches, the central one much than the others, and with the remains of a minar on each side of it. Each arch is surrounded by lines of writing, the outer in Kufic, and the other two in the Arabic character, and divided from each by bands of Arabesque ornament, the whole boldly and clearly cut in a hard yellow limestone, discc indeed, but still as sharp as on the day it was erected.

On the lower belt of writing on the north minar, General Cunningham was able to read in 18‹ words—

"Saltân-us Sulatin-us-Shark . . . Abu-ul-Muzafar Ailtamish us Sultâne Nâser Amir-ul Mûminîn:"

which go to prove that the masjid was completed in the reign of Altamish, A.D. 1211 to 1236; the back wall, under the roof of one of the domes, he found a Kufic inscription in two lines, which, incomplete at the beginning, has been restored and rendered:—

"*This masjid was built* during the guardianship of Akbar, the son of Ahmad, *by the help of G* Creator, the Everlasting, in the month Zi-hijjah, five hundred and ninety-six." (Sept. A.D. 1200.) And really belonged originally to this mosk, it would show that it was built in A.D. 1200.

"In gorgeous prodigality of ornament, in beautiful richness of tracery, and endless variety of de‹ delicate sharpness of finish, and laborious accuracy of workmanship, all of which are due to the masons," General Cunningham remarks, the two great mosks of Dehli and Ajneer "may justly vie w noblest buildings which the world has yet produced." This estimate is perhaps somewhat exaggerate not much if restricted to the screen, of which it is to be regretted there is no adequate representatior

---

* See Tod, *Annals*, vol. i. pp. 778—782 (Mad. ed. pp. 665—669); Cunningham, *Reports*, vol. ii. pp. 258 *seqq.*; and Fergusson, *Hist. Architect.* vol. ii. pp. 646—650.

XXVII. JAYPUR, FROM THE SANGANER GATE.

JAYPUR.

Photograph XXVII.

JAYPUR, the capital of the Rajput state of the same name, is about 144 miles west from Agra, and was founded by Râja Siwai Jay Singh in 1728. This prince, who ruled from 1698 to 1742, was equally remarkable for his intellectual capacity, his patronage of science and art, and his architectural skill. The great Observatory—constructed according to his own plans, and still tolerably entire—and those erected at Dehli, Banâras and Ujjain, are proofs of his devotion to astronomy and of his advanced skill and knowledge. With these he was enabled to base upon the tables of De la Hire, and to leave as a lasting monument of his industry and acquirements, the tables known as the *Zij Muhammad shahi.*

The city of Jayapur was founded as his new capital, in place of Amber, a few miles to the north of it, and was laid out by him on a regular plan of six great blocks in two rows of three each, divided by main streets 110 feet wide, intersecting at right angles. One block in the centre of the second row is given up to the palace, and behind this again are the lakes. The blocks are intersected by secondary streets 55 feet wide, and from these minor streets, 27½ feet broad, diverge at right angles,. "At the end of each of the main streets are the gates—six in number—handsome, lofty masonry structures, exactly similar to one another. The walls round the city are lofty, of masonry and crenellated, but without ramparts, and not intended for guns, or to resist artillery, the real defence against an invading force being the detached forts and the hills forts which surround the place." The main streets are each of one colour, red, green, blue, yellow, &c., and the shops are all similar, being of masonry with colonnaded verandas, and "the whole city bears the impress of the genius of the sovereign who founded it."

The population, exclusive of the suburbs, which may contain 40,000, is estimated at 160,000.

The gates—as is usual in Indian cities—are named after the chief towns to which the road from each leads. Eight miles to the south is Sânganer, and hence the gate leading to it goes by that name. The panoramic views of the city from over this gate are very fine; seldom can an Indian city be so well seen from a single point, and few cities are more beautiful, or more regularly built, than Jaypur. It is situated in a small plain,—which Heber describes as resembling a "large estuary, but studded with rocky islands, whose sands were left here by the receding tide,"—and has, on all sides except the south, barren, rocky hills, crowned in many cases by forts. The citadel is built on a hill to the north that rises several hundred feet above the town, and "has a very bold appearance when viewed from the town, the south face of the rocks being very precipitous, and totally inaccessible." *

---

* See Tod, *Annals*, vol. ii. pp. 356—368 (Mad. ed. pp. 328—339); Heber's *Journal*, vol. ii. pp. 31 *seqq.*; *Selections from the Records of Govt. of India*, No. lxv. pp. 8, 9; Sutherland, *Sketches*, pp. 74—77; Jacquemont, *Voyages*, vol. vi. pp. 364—373; Boileau, *Tour in Rajwara*, pp. 157—159; *Asiat. Res.* vol. v. p. 185 *seqq.*; *Orient. Mag.* vol. viii. p. 18; Malcolm, *Cent. India*, vol. ii. p. 126; Briggs' *Ferishta*, vol. i. p. 343, vol. ii. p. 260; Erskine Perry's *Bird's Eye View of India*, p. 142.

THE INDUR MEHAL AT JAYPUR.

Photograph XXVIII.

AS already mentioned, the palace, with its gardens, &c., occupies the central block of buildings in the being about half a mile in length. The principal front is seven or eight stories high, and is flar at each end by a lofty tower surmounted by a cupola. Within are two very spacious courts, several of smaller dimensions, surrounded by fully a dozen different palaces, communicating with other by corridors or gardens. The large garden is extremely beautiful, and is kept up with much taste. most remarkable of the palaces are the Diwân-i Khâs, or Hall of Audience, which contains a splendid ob saloon, built entirely of white marble; and the Indur Mehâl in the garden, where levees and public recept and dinners are held.

XXVIII. JAYPUR, THE INDUR MEHAL.

XXIX. THE GALTA, NEAR JAYPUR.

THE GALTÂ.

Photograph XXIX.

GALTÂ is a sacred place, three miles east of Jaypur, bearing somewhat the same relation to Jaypur as Eklinga does to Udaypur. Ḍhunḍhâ was an Asura, or demon king. It is said that Visal Deva of Ajmer, for his oppression of his subjects, and at the curse of a bania's daughter, an ascetic at Pushkar, whom he forced in the midst of her penances, after his death from the bite of a snake became an Asura, an eater of the flesh of men; "searching," says the Bard Chand, "he ate men, thence his name Ḍhunḍhâ"—from *ḍhûnḍhnâ* 'to search.' He was reclaimed from this life by his grandson offering himself as a victim to his insatiable appetite, and afterwards lived in the cave or rather fissure in the rock near the top of the hill at Galtâ, performing penance for his wickedness. From him, or this cave, the rivulet below was named the Ḍhunḍhu, and the country on its banks Ḍhunḍhuvâra or Ḍhunḍhâr—the native appellation of the Jaypur territory previous to the seventeenth century. In the Purâṇas it is said that on being attacked by Kuvalâyâsva, the Asura Ḍhunḍhâ—but perhaps not the same as Visal Deva—hid himself beneath a sea of sand, which was dug up by Kuvalâyâsva and his twenty-one sons, in spite of the anger of the monster, who, by his fiery breath, consumed eighteen of them,—a legend which, General Cunningham suggests, may be connected with the vast sandy plains along both banks of the Ḍhunḍhu river, from which the wind raises clouds of smokelike dust.*

---

* See Tod, *Rajasthan*, vol. ii. pp. 345 *seqq.* (Mad. ed. pp. 318 *seqq.*); *Indian Antiquary*, vol. i. pp. 278 *seqq.*; Cunningham's *Reports*, vol. ii. p. 251.

AMBER.

Photograph XXX.

THE capital of the State, before the foundation of Jaypur, was Amber. It is about five miles to the no east of the present capital and quite shut in by surrounding hills, but is almost entirely deserted now, numerous trees grow in its unfrequented streets and ruined courts. "La ville d'Amber," as Jacquen remarks, is "tombe en ruine; on dirait une cité marquée par une providence funeste, visitée par une fl destructeur. Pas un habitant, pas une voix, que le murmure monotone de la prière d'un Brahmane r fidèle à quelqu'un des vieux temples." At the south end of the town is a small lake or ta and on its margin are the royal baths. A steep ascent leads from these up to the castle or pal which contains numerous courts and suites of apartments, some of them small and reached thro intricate passages, others extremely beautiful, "and enjoying from their windows, balconies, and terraces, of the most striking prospects which can be conceived." One of the most highly ornamented of the build here is the Kanch Mehal, or Glass Palace—so called, because much of its interior is decorated with look glass inserted in the wainscoting of the walls. The windows of it are of perforated marble work—without m variety in the patterns, perhaps, but beautifully carved, and which has a peculiarly pleasing effect inside. the left of the view is seen a corner of a noble open hall of audience. The floors and all the pillars, ex those on the three outer sides, are of white or yellowish white marble; the outer line, however, are of red sandst and of quite a different pattern: they are double-columns, and at the corners quadruple, connected, and of purely Musalman pattern, resembling a slender baluster. This had, doubtless, been tried for effect, but contrast both in colour and form being unpleasant, these outer pillars have been plastered over with ma chunam, in such a way as to bring them nearly into perfect accordance in form and colour with the marble colu inside. This reason, however, has been lost sight of, and an impossible legend invented to account for disguised form of the sandstone pillars. The Padshah of Dehli, they say, hearing of the beauty of these sl in the audience hall of Jaysingh, sent masons and others to Amber to secure copies of them for a new pa for the Mughul, and the Mahârâja, unwilling to allow their being copied, had them at once covered over plaster in the way they now are.

"For myself," says Heber, "I have seen many royal palaces containing larger and more stately roon many, the architecture of which was in purer taste, and some which have covered a greater extent of gr (though in *this*, if the fortress on the hill be included, Amber will rank, I think, above Windsor),—but varied and picturesque effect, for richness of carving, for wild beauty of situation, for the number and rom singularity of the apartments, and the strangeness of finding such a building in such a place and country, I able to compare nothing with Amber; and this, too, was the work of Jaysingh!* The ornaments are in same style, though in a better taste, than those of his palace at Jaypur, and the size and number of apartments are also similar. A greater use has been made of stained glass here, or else from the inacces height of the window the glass has remained in better preservation. The building is in good repair, but a solitary and deserted aspect; and as our guide, with his bunch of keys, unlocked one iron-clenched door another, and led us over terraces and up towers, down steep, dark, sloping passages, and through a

* This is perhaps in part a mistake, or the work of Jaysingh I., A.D. 1625 has been attributed to his more illustrious successor Jaysin A.D. 1698—1742.

XXX. AMBER—THE KANCH MEHAL.

succession of silent courts and dim vaulted chambers, seen only through coloured glass, and made more gorgeously gloomy by their carving, gilding, and mirrors, the idea of an enchanted castle occurred, I believe, to us all."

Nor is it much changed at the present day. Jacquemont says of it: "Je n'ai rien vu de si pittoresque en Europe, parmi ce que le moyen âge nous a laissé de ruines. Amber d'ailleurs, qui a tout le charme triste d'une ruine, n'en est pas une. Il n'y a qu'un siècle qu'il a cessé d'être la résidence du Radjah de Jeïpour, et depuis la fondation de la ville nouvelle, il est constamment entretenu, et par intervalles habité par les descendants de Jeï-Sing, qui sont justement fiers de ce magnifique monument de l'ancienne splendeur de leur maison. Ce n'est pas un palais; c'est une ville de palais unis les uns aux autres pour former un système de défense commune. Au gré des accidents du sol, ses murailles s'élèvent ou s'abaissent, se couronnent de créneaux élégants ou se percent seulement des rares meurtrières, enfin se dressent comme les escarpements des rochers, là où l'inaccessibilité de leur base leur sert suffisamment de défense."

Within this palace is a shrine of Kâlî—the goddess of destruction—where a kid is sacrificed daily. Tradition reports that, in olden time, human victims were offered here, but the custom had become obsolete until Jaysingh was frightened by a dream in which Kâlî appeared to him demanding why her image was left unsatisfied with blood to quench her thirst. The Mahârâja by advice "substituted a goat for the human victim, with which the

'Dark goddess of the azure flood,
Whose robes are wet with infant tears,
Skull-chaplet wearer, whom the blood
Of man delights three thousand years,'

was graciously pleased to be contented."*

* See Heber's *Journal*, vol. ii. pp. 39, 40; Tod's *Rajasthan*, vol. ii. pp. 345 *seqq.* and 438 (Mad. ed. pp. 318 *seqq.* and 404; Jacquemont, *Voyage dans l'Inde*, tome iii. pp. 375—377.